MW00874734

POISED

With Bride Mentality

By

SUSIE PURKEY

Copyright © 2014 by Susie Purkey

Poised
With Bride Mentality
by Susie Purkey

Printed in the United States of America
ISBN 9781629521404

All rights reserved solely by the author. The author guarantees all contents are original and do not infringe upon the legal rights of any other person or work. No part of this book may be reproduced in any form without the permission of the author. The views expressed in this book are not necessarily those of the publisher.

Unless otherwise indicated, Bible quotations are taken from the New Living Version (NLT). Copyright, 1966. Used by permission of Tyndale House Publishers, Inc. Wheaton, Illinois 60189. All rights reserved.

Cover Photo Credit: Picture entitled "ARRIVAL", created July 11, 2012. Courtesy of: Prophetic Arts of James Nesbit, New Baden, Illinois. www.jamesnart.net

> "As the Great King descends from the heavens in this magnificent room…The King is close enough to His beloved bride that she can feel the warmth of His breath. He is here in the room; the moment they have longed for through eternity. He has come!"

*Please check out the web-site of Mr. James Nesbit. He is a gifted and anointed Artist and has many works of art available for purchase. James is a gift to the body of Christ and I would like to thank him publicly, for working with me.

www.xulonpress.com

To my *Beloved,* Mark:
"Much of what I have learned about how Christ loves
His Church has come from the way you have loved me.
Thank you for believing in me.

*"Christ loved the church. He gave up His life for her to
make her holy and clean, washed by the cleansing of
God's Word. He did this to present her to Himself as
a glorious church without spot or wrinkle or any other
blemish. Instead, she will be holy and without fault. In
the same way, husbands ought to love their wives as
they love their own bodies. For a man who loves his
wife actually shows love for himself."*
Ephesians 5:25-28 (NLV)

And To My Beloved Children,
**Lucas Mark, Andrea Elizabeth (Gray)
and Lyndi Marie Purkey**
And My Beloved Grandchildren and Future
Grandchildren:
Beckham Luke and Haven Elizabeth Purkey
I leave you This Legacy…Let's All Finish Strong"!
With all my Love, **Nina**

TABLE OF CONTENTS

PREFACE

I never aspired to write a book.

Singing was always "my thing" and I started out by singing on the radio at the age of eight, in the third grade. My father was stationed at the military base in Camp Lejeune, North Carolina. The year was 1966. I sang "Somewhere over the Rainbow", for my elementary school's Spring Concert and to my surprise, received a standing ovation from the audience and a gleaming silver dollar from the Commanding Officer of the Marine Base, who was present that night. Later, it was decided to broadcast the performance on the local radio. I guess that's when I first knew that I could sing.

I would go on to study music as a career choice at Southeastern Assemblies of God University, in Lakeland, Florida, majoring in Vocal Music Performance with a minor in Biblical Studies and eventually graduating in 1982, after a transfer to Central Bible College (CBC), in Springfield, Missouri. There, at CBC, destiny would put me on the radio again, this time singing for the National Radio Broadcasting Choir of the Assemblies of God, (aka **Revivaltime Choir**). I was honored to be a Soloist for that organization, for four years.

Since then, it has been my pleasure and honor to be a Music Director and vocal instructor to hundreds of students throughout our thirty two years of full-time ministry. I have **loved** teaching others to sing, especially my own children! However, my *number one* is STILL ministering in music, in the local church with my awesome Guy, Missionary Evangelist, Mark R. Purkey. We've be so privileged to travel the world, preaching the Gospel of our Lord Jesus Christ together. And in the past thirty two years, we have ministered to roughly 1.5 million people and seen more than 100,000 decisions made for Christ and we give **all the glory to God**.

No, I never planned on writing a book. However, in January, 2012, right after my dad passed away, I felt a strong urgency to write a book about my dramatic Back Story of growing up in a third-generation alcoholic family, Mark's dramatic healing of Lymphoma Cancer, at the age of nineteen, and that of my fifteen year prayer-journey of believing God to save and deliver my dad from alcohol addiction and demonic oppression. In essence, a book about the many miraculous stories of our lives.

However, not wanting the book to just be about "me and mine", I decided to develop a Theme and Bible Study that I could incorporate along with it. It would have a Study-Guide application for use by individuals and local church groups. My desire, Dear Reader, is to improve our "corporate readiness", concerning the imminent return of Jesus Christ. **Bride Mentality, as it relates to Jesus' Bride-Church, is a gender-neutral term because we know that the Church is made up of Men *and* Women.** Therefore, men **and** women are called the "Bride of Christ" and this book applies to both genders.

Human beings all possess a genetic blueprint. It's called our *GENOME*. A person's genome functions as a biological instruction manual or a genetic book. In essence, it's what makes us "tic".[1] It's important to note, however, that from a spiritual standpoint, God has a plan for a person's life *beyond the plan written in their genetic code*. How exciting!

"For I know the plans I have for you," says the Lord. "They are plans for good and not for disaster, to give you a future and a hope." [2]

Now, using the above scripture as a pivoting point, let's imagine what the genetic blueprint of the Bride of Christ, might look like! If we could describe her genetic code, using a list of characteristics, that simplification could be a *valuable teaching tool in the church today!* So, I have adapted an **ACRONYM** for the purpose of our study and we will call it **P.O.I.S.E.D.**

This is a 6-Part Study and I highly recommend the companion Study-Guide (released summer of 2014), that accompanies this book, for growth in all areas of your spiritual life. Here are a few areas that "**POISED with Bride Mentality**" will help you with:

- Do you lack victory and long to have peace of mind that you're really "Saved"?
- Do you wish that you could pray more powerful prayers but don't know how?
- Are you struggling with Obedience and letting go of Secret Sins? Do you have Habits that you're not proud of?

- Is there personal Integrity in your life concerning your money, relationships and your reputation? If not, learn how to improve.

- How can you become "Addicted to God's Word"? Learning how to be "Well-Studied", and have a desire to read His Love Letters, gives you the upper hand with the devil.

- Where are your affections? What are you looking at? Who's your Number One? (Is it *YOU*?) This book will help you find out WHERE your "Eyes are Focused".

- Do you take Dominion every day of your life, subduing your enemy with the Authority of Christ? *"Are you Dressed to Kill?"* If you're weak in this area, learn how to KNOW **WHO** YOU ARE IN CHRIST and how to fight Spiritual Warfare!

I've been writing for two years and it's been like giving birth.

(Ah Hem) …sleepless nights with my baby in my arms, travailing prayer and every waking moment with my trusty i-notes-in-hand, so as to **not** miss a single "God-whisper". You know… the blood, sweat and tears thing. And *Voila'*, the result is in your hand! (Angelic Choir Sound) I can hardly believe it and boy am I glad this baby finally came. (Here's to clinking my coffee cup with you now!)

This for me has been more about "obedience to the Spirit's voice", than anything else. It has been an Exercise in Listening and Ahhhh! It has truly brought me peace and fulfillment. Don't you just love Peace? And I have to say, there has been a paradigm shift that has occurred in me. I confess that I *LOVE* writing now too! Maybe I'll write more books... Regardless, as long as I'm able, I'll continue singing, ministering and traveling evangelistically throughout the world, with my awesome Guy and now, when I do, I will have a new prospective to talk about... how to be: **POISED**!

*Calling All Church-Brides! Have you heard? There's going to be a BIG, FAT, HEAVENLY WEDDING and **IF** you're wearing the right attire...you're ALL INVITED! Now, Let's Get Engaged!*

KEY TEXT

THE PARABLE OF THE TEN VIRGINS (Matthew 25: 1-13)

"*T*hen the Kingdom of Heaven will be like ten brides-maids who took their lamps and went out to meet the bridegroom. Five of them were foolish and five were wise. The five who were foolish didn't take enough olive oil for their lamps. But the other five were wise enough to take along extra oil. When the bridegroom was delayed, they all became drowsy and fell asleep. At midnight they were roused by the shout, "Look, the bridegroom is coming! Come out and meet him!"

All the bridesmaids got up and prepared their lamps. Then the five foolish ones asked the others, "Please give us some of your oil because our lamps are going out."

But the others replied, "We don't have enough for all of us. Go to the shop and buy some for yourselves." But while they were gone to buy oil, the bridegroom came. Then, those who were ready, went in with Him to the marriage feast and the door was locked. Later, when the other five bridesmaids returned, they stood outside calling, "Lord! Lord! Open the door for us!"

But He called back, "Believe me, I don't know you!"

"So you too, must keep watch! For you do not know the day or hour of my return." **(Words spoken by Jesus)**

FORWARD

*T*he Lord Jesus is coming back for a Bride-Church without spot or wrinkle, washed in the blood of the Lamb. Now, picture with me a beautiful wedding scene. OH! The splendor of it all...the cathedral, the flowers, the wedding party shimmering in the finest attire; the Guests all assembled, likewise, in their "Sunday Best". *EXPECTANT.*

Now, picture the Groom, front and center, standing at attention in full regal dress. He's fresh, pressed, groomed down to his fingernails and ready to see the Love of His Life! His "pick". Just then, the back door of the Grand Sanctuary opens...Enter **Bridezilla.** (People GASP)

Her dress is filthy. There are visible spots on it everywhere. The lace is torn at the bottom and many sequins are missing. In fact, *she* is dirty. She didn't bother to even bathe and her hair looks like she's been through a tornado! She casually schleps down the aisle. The guests gasp in horror and whisper among themselves, *"Is she out of her mind?"* Perhaps.

This would-be-bride is *so distracted* by *everything* and *everybody* else in the room, that her EYES never even meet that of her Grooms. She never even looks at him! Caught up in all the pleasures and allurements around her, she ignores the most important person in the room... her Bride-Groom. Now, here's the million dollar question:

"Who in their right mind, would want to marry ***THAT BRIDE?***

Exactly.

She's the ultimate *"Bridezilla"*. Her affections are misplaced and the groom knows from her behavior that she doesn't **really** love him. He's not "first-place" in her life and everyone else in the room knows it as well. The Groom's face flushes with embarrassment and he walks away, shutting the door behind him. The Wedding is "OFF"! (Fade to Black)

Now, I'm sure many of you are already ahead of me, making the spiritual parallel and the truth is, *there is one!* Dear Reader, this is a sad but true picture of today's Luke-warm Church. There are millions of people today, who profess to be Christian, who rarely attend church services, read the Bible, or pray (unless there is some huge disaster).

They don't support, they don't serve, and they don't show!

Yes, I kid you not…Millions.

But still, these people think they are going to go to heaven when they die. (Cricket-cricket)

Seriously?

Let me say this *delicately.* "We Have A Problem Here".

Can I be candid? My husband and I travel. *A LOT.* Three million miles with one air-carrier alone, at last count and that doesn't even include trains, automobiles and pack animals! We have visited and ministered in, more than twenty foreign countries in the last thirty years, as Missionary Evangelists with the Assemblies of God. And as I stated previously, we've personally ministered to over a million and a half people in the U.S. and overseas and are literally in a different church venue every week. So, please believe me when I tell you, we see "Luke-warm"! And it is **breaking** our hearts.

The would-be Church-Bride is sick. We see spiritual anemia everywhere. Despite a surge in dynamic Praise and Worship accompanied by musical excellence, many church congregations are spiritually weak, apathetic, sickly, under fed spiritually, speaking negatively, gambling in casinos, full of alcoholics with alcohol drinking becoming more and more common-place in; **on** and **off-campus** church meetings and Moral failures...well, they are at an all-time high, **in** and **out** of the pulpit. (God Forbid)

It's just like the picture of "Bridezilla", isn't it? This is a fictitious name I have created to help you understand, the Luke-warm church. If she *really* loved the bridegroom, then she would have made every effort to present herself in a manner worthy of him! She would have carried herself the way someone truly devoted and in LOVE does and she would have had EYES only for Him.

Jesus said, "Why do you call me Lord, Lord and do not do the things that I say?" [3]

The Luke-warm place is the most dangerous place for us to be in. And yet, by-in-large, the Church today, is plagued by a form of Godliness but we have no REAL, power of God, evident in many of our lives or services. In the words of one Old-time preacher, "We couldn't get a fly healed of a headache!" *Why?*

"It's about No Oil in Our Lamps", Dear Reader.

Throughout the Old and New Testaments, oil is symbolic of the anointing and of Joy. (aka, the Oil of Gladness). Did you know that the lamp represents our lives? Let's put the two together. When the Holy Spirit is filling us inside (oil), we possess an anointing and a power for His service. He fills our lamp or life. It's as simple as that. Even children in children's church can understand this. We have a little song, we teach them that says,

"This little light of mine. I'm gonna let it shine. Let it shine. Let it shine. Let it shine!"

We must be burning brightly for Jesus Christ when He returns for us. Verse 3 of Matthew 25, says:

"The foolish bridesmaids brought their lamps but not enough oil to last thru the night."

The night represents our waiting period until Jesus returns. What happens at nighttime? We get drowsy. Absence of light makes one sleepy. When you get sleepy, you also get cold, that's why we cover up.

It's the same way, spiritually.

When we are not waiting, watching and working. When we are not burning brightly for Jesus, when we **let** our lamps go out…we get Luke-warm. I said, **"We LET"**, *it is an act of our voluntary will.* No excuses.

However, if we are wise and prepared, like the five wise bridesmaids who brought extra oil in case the bridegroom was delayed; then that extra anointing helps **propel** *us through trials.* It helps **propel** *us through hardships.* It helps **propel** *us through anything life dishes out!* It provides the *illumination* we need to be awake when He returns and calls for us!

Then, we will be rewarded with **ACCESS.** The highly coveted, All-Access Pass, into the Marriage Supper. (Vs.10) says it will be a *great* feast. And then the door will be locked and there will be no further admittance. Jesus our Bridegroom awaits the Father's final triumphant command:

"Go, Bring My Children Home!"

And when this final declaration is finally made, the bible says that there will be a great trumpet BLAST! Millions of blood-washed Christians, who have been waiting, watching and staying prepared with the oil of anointing in their lamps, will be "Raptured" or "Caught Away". (2Corinthians 15:52)

In the twinkling of an eye, the bible says. That's pretty quick, folks. Blink. That's how quick! That is why there will not be any extra time to **get** ready. If you're not already ready, it will be too late. I have to say this is a HUGE motivator for me. That, and hearing those two, ALL-IMPORTANT words from the lips of Jesus, *"Well done!"* (Oh, how I long to hear them!)

You see, we can't afford to get sleepy and luke-warm, friends. It's a trap. But many pastors and church leaders, today, are caught up in running big numbers, *at the expense of the TRUTH*. Deleting (by not preaching), parts of the Gospel message about Sin, Repentance and Regeneration, for fear of offending someone is wrong. *It's called the Sin of Omission.* Unfortunately, this is one of the latest trends in Christendom and its killing the Church. It's creating "Bridezilla."

If you're reading this and you are involved in Church leadership, I appeal to you to *TEACH THE WHOLE GOSPEL OF OUR LORD JESUS CHRIST*. This is what keeps us in line. If we are lulled to sleep by a watered- down gospel that **omits** ultimatums, consequences of sin and teachings about Hell, then we've fallen prey to a trap set there by the enemy of God himself. Satan. He is the enemy of all our souls and millions could be doomed, just like the five foolish or unwise bridesmaids…simply by *not being prepared*.

WANTED! BRIDEZILLA…NOT ARMED! NOT DANGEROUS!

(Ah Hem), She drifts into church occasionally–taking up space on a pew. At offering time, she throws an insignificant offering (one that involves no sacrifice; it's not about the amount), into the plate, to appease her guilty conscience and leaves the same way she came in! She wouldn't think of missing a worship concert but **never** darkens the door for a prayer function, or church work day. This is just the type of person who thinks they are going to heaven but they're **NOT**!

"How Can You Judge? I can just hear some people say", that are reading this.

*I'm not. I'm heralding the words of **Jesus, himself*** *to stir the sleeping!*

To reiterate, one of the purposes of this book is to **Improve Corporate Readiness** for the imminent return of our Lord. Listen to **Jesus'** solemn words from Matthew 7:21. (NLT)

> *"Not everyone who calls out to me, 'Lord, Lord', will enter the Kingdom of Heaven. Only those who actually do the will of my Father in heaven will enter."*

These foolish ones fall asleep, listening to the cadence of the world. Feeding off of materialism and pleasure-madness...their lamps go OUT. Then, when the Sound of Heaven occurs, announcing Jesus, our Bridegroom has arrived; they'll never even hear it because they are sound asleep... Spiritually. (Zzz) And, by the time they stir around and realize that He's come and gone, it will be too late. They will have been left behind. It's **so** Sad. Don't let this be you, Dear Reader! Let us shake ourselves!

No one gets a free-pass on servant-hood. (Especially the Leadership), We're all required to work in His Harvest fields. This is how the Kingdom of God works.

I'll always be grateful to God for my Uncle David. He pestered me to go to church with him for months (before I did), not knowing the personal struggles of my drug use, deep depression and suicide attempt at the age of fourteen. Thank God, he wouldn't take "NO" for an answer, or I might not be here today. I tell the story of my conversion in Chapter One. God used him in my life and I commemorate my Uncle, David Hammond here, in this book, for leading me to Christ. "Thank you, Uncle Dave."

I'll say it again, "We Must All Be Working For The Lord".

So how do we receive our degree in <u>Bride Mentology 101</u>? (Insert wink here).

Well, for starters, you need to get P.O.I.S.E.D...Read on!

~~~BRIDE MENTALITY~~~

PART ONE

P. IS FOR POWERFUL IN PRAYER

O.

I.

S.

E.

D.

Chapter One~

A RAISED-UP WOMAN~

We're Not Called to Just Sit Around the Palace and Look Pretty…

"Unless the Lord had helped me, I would soon have settled in the silence of the grave." Psalm 94:17 (NLV)

I wasn't raised in a Christian home, per se. We attended church on Christmas and Easter, like most American families. My mother was raised Southern Baptist, my father grew up in a Catholic orphanage, so I like to say they compromised and went to the First Church of "No Where". Maybe you've heard of it.

My father, Lawrence Neal McGrath, was a second generation alcoholic and the youngest of fifteen children. He hid his drinking problem from my mother before their marriage. The US Navy drafted him straight out of the Catholic orphanage in Tampa, Florida where he enlisted at the ripe old age of seventeen and a half. It didn't take long for this young man, with no family roots to ground him, to succumb to peer-pressure and start drinking alcohol; in order to cope with the pressures of war.

The Korean War of 1945-1953 was in full swing at the time and dad was wounded in battle there, when he took shrapnel fire from a bullet, in his leg. Later, he would receive the Purple Heart, Medal of Honor for his service in Korea but was sent home to recuperate from his injuries. He met my mother at a dance on the military base in Jacksonville, Florida and they were married on April 16, 1957. They were 23 and 22 years old, respectively. Together they had four children of which I am the eldest.

As a child, I remember attending the Mandarin Baptist Church in Jacksonville, Florida with my maternal grandparents. It seemed I was always drawn to God. At the age of seven, I became aware of my need of a Savior one Sunday morning, so I left the comfort of my padded pew to walk the aisle alone and knelt at the altar of that Southern Baptist Church. The year was 1965. I was water baptized a few weeks later. However, with no encouragement in my home life, to attend church and to grow in my new faith, I was greatly hindered and eventually fell away from the things of the Lord. This was exacerbated by the fact that my military family moved so often that I attended thirteen schools in my twelve years of formative education. We were constantly being transferred to new locations and my father's drinking problem became **all** of ours to deal with.

Consequently, by the time I was just fourteen years of age, my parents divorced and we four children stayed with our sweet mother, Sylvia. Being the eldest child of four and under the care of only a single parent, brought new challenges and life was hard. I fell into a deep depression. Ashamed of where we lived and feeling the stigma of divorce, poverty and lack, I became hopeless that my life would ever turn into anything good or that our family circumstances would ever change.

So, in March of 1973, in the bathroom of our small home, (pictured on my Chapter One Title page), I took a blunt-ended kitchen object and tried to take my own life. I had fallen into street drugs and was smoking pot and cigarettes and earlier that year; I had been arrested for shoplifting and spent a night in the Juvenile Detention Center, in downtown Jacksonville. The depression was choking me and pulling me down, in to a pit. I was suffocating everyday of shame, anger and resentment against my father because he left us.

Convinced now, that this was the only way to end my pain, I stood there in that desperate moment of eternity, with trembling hands. Looking at my reflection in the mirror, over the rust-stained, sink, I was all alone. That's when I heard it.

The sound of a voice…but there was no one else in the room?

No other sound, except the steady drip of water, to muffle my sobs. I couldn't tell if it was audible but it seemed deafening to me. There were only three words spoken.

*The voice said, **"You'll Never Know!"***

They were only *three **little** words* but *three **powerful** words that* shot through the locked door of my darkness and depression and temporarily interrupted my attempted suicide. *"I'll Never Know"*, I queried? "What does that even mean? *What is it, that I'll Never Know?"*

Instantly, a divine curiosity was piqued in me. I had all but lost my childhood curiosity when I had to face adult things too early. It had been robbed from me... but God put it back!

He's Good At That.

It was one of the defining moments of my life. Isn't it interesting what the Spirit of God says to us at defining moments of our lives? I'm fascinated by that. At the moment, I didn't know it was **God**, speaking to me but time would reveal that it was. Confused, I ran out of that small, dingy bathroom but my depression, anger and deep despair were still very much intact.

As I mentioned in my **FORWARD**, my Uncle Dave had been pestering me for over a year, to attend a youth gathering with him. Just five years older than I, he was always more like a big brother to me; so, temporarily shaken in my resolve to have nothing to do with God, I now reluctantly agreed to attend the youth service with him. As I stated previously, the year was 1973 and a historic movement was taking place in the United States of America. Wikipedia describes it as follows:

*"**The Jesus Movement** was a movement in Christianity beginning on the West Coast of the United States in the late 1960s and early 1970s and spreading primarily through North America and Europe, before dying out by the early 1980s. It was the major Christian element within the hippie counterculture, or, conversely, the major hippie element with some strands of Protestantism, Members of the movement were called Jesus people or Jesus freaks."*

So, I found myself in a little non-denominational Coffee-House called, **"The House of the Risen Son"** and was shocked by what I encountered there. No dead, dry religion here! No big ole pipe organ or even stained glass...just kids sitting around on the floors, playing guitars and singing their hearts out for Jesus. There *was* a message spoken that night, but I don't remember it. What I **DO** remember was the love I felt. It was strong and undeniable. That night, I felt the hand of God touch me **after** the service, in the parking lot!

We were just leaning around on the cars, talking, when out of nowhere, I began sobbing; unable to hold it in, any longer because I had so much "crud", pent up inside of me. So many layers of hatred and hurt, anger and anxiety but they all had to give way that night, to the powerful, unseen hand of God. The power of the cross is greater than all our sin! He delivered me and washed over me with His surpassing peace. I felt the chains fall at my feet. My friends all gathered around, praying for me. Feeling their hands of support, on my shoulders, I felt the undeniable love of God through them.

Then the JOY came. Joy unspeakable and full of glory, as the old song says. They told me later that I ran around in circles, throughout that sandy, homemade, Florida parking lot with my hands raised; crying and shouting the praises of God. I don't actually remember running. But, somewhere under those old Live Oaks, with their heavy laden branches of Spanish moss, I came to my senses again and realized I had been delivered. Yes, I had met Jesus! He came in and filled all the deep caverns of my soul. His light and love washed over me and splashed up and over the sides of my life. My eyes leaked. It was undeniably, tangibly, powerfully, REAL.

And the proof?

From that day forward, I was never the same. I never looked back. And even though I love my family with all my heart, I am so vastly different from most of my family members, that I often jokingly say, "I must have been switched at the hospital!" *My life course was **"altered by the altar"** and I was on my way to a better life.*

- How about You? What bondage has God delivered you of, that no longer entices you? Think about it. In my companion Study-Guide, I give space and attention to journaling your journey, as I have just done. We overcome by the Word of our Testimony (Back Story) and by the blood of Jesus. Take time to Overcome!

- Were your robbed of something? Has God put it back? Why not? Have you allowed Him too? Another purpose of this book is to tell you that God's arm is not too short, to reach you…to heal or save or redeem what the devil has stolen from you. **Let Him Put It Back!**

Pray this prayer with me right now. "Father, I come to you in the name of Jesus. I confess Him as my Lord and Savior and ask you to forgive me of my sins. I know He died on the cross to give me eternal, abundant life. I've fallen into a pit of despair and right now, I'm not enjoying abundant life and I feel like I have been violated. Please restore my inner child. My child-like faith, please Restore to me the Joy of my salvation in you." I loose you to work in my life! In Jesus name, Amen!"

MARRIAGE SUCCESS~

I love weddings! The very word congers up excitement! Everyone loves to see a couple on the "cusp of their future", tie the knot. Yes, weddings always touch my heart. It seems nearly everyone starts out committed and their excitement is, well...contagious!

Jesus went away two thousand years ago and when He did, He said to His disciples,

"There is more than enough room in my Father's house. I go to prepare a place for you. When everything is ready, I will come and get you, so that you will always be with me, where I am. [5]

35

(Holy Moly!) This has turned out to be *the longest courtship in history.* So just **how do** we keep that "Lov'in Feeling"…that Divine Expectation?

It's about staying ***P.O.I.S.E.D.***

Marriage success is determined largely by your partner's commitment. I'd say 50 % is about right. In fact, you can be 100% committed to the union but if you don't have a partner that meets you half way, you're almost always doomed for failure. In fact, according to the *2010 Census Bureau, The National Center for Family and Marriage Research* and *The Journal for Marriage and Family,* analysis indicates that the probability of marriage ending in divorce increased linearly throughout the 20th Century and reached a plateau in the 1990s with the most recent estimate (for the year 2000), indicating that 45% of marriages would end in divorce. If we take into account the fact that a small percentage of marriages end in permanent separation, rather than divorce, then the overall rate of union disruption is slightly less than 50%.[6]

In other words, the commonly cited statistic: that about half of all marriages end in disruption; (divorce or permanent separation), appears to be reasonably accurate. So, marriage is a two-way proposal.

Currently, I've been married for thirty-two years, to the same person. So, I know a little about having a "Bride-Mentality", in the earthly sense. However, I know that many of you, Dear Readers, find it difficult to get excited about the marriage to our bridegroom Jesus, because you have *"issues with the one you've got"!* (Insert wink here) Perhaps, you've lost the excitement and desire for one another and for the future. You're tired and you've been disappointed. I get that. I came from a broken home, FULL of unfaithfulness, disappointment and divorce.

But don't blame Jesus for this and think that *He's the same kind of marriage partner*, because He's not!

Can I just propose to you, that *that* "Mindset Overlap," will hinder us and creep in to, the *Bride-Mentality Mindset* that we need to have for our heavenly Bridegroom? And if we allow it to, *it will rob us of many things, included in a Blessed Life!*

I'm inviting you to re-think *EVERYTHING* you've ever thought about marriage, setting aside pre-conceived ideas. Let's take the "Limits Off." I will break this topic down even further in PART 5–EYES FOCUSED, but for now, try and detach from your current marriage ideals or any negative viewpoints you may have on the subject; because as I have said, some of you have been very hurt by your marriage(s) and therefore may have an unintentional bias on the subject.

This can prevent you from receiving all God has for us!

Jesus paid the ultimate price to show His love for us–**by giving "His Life for His Wife"**, so-to-speak. The Church *IS* His Bride. There is no greater love than that. He showed His level of commitment by going to the Cross. He's the *Lover of Our Souls* and we'll **never** have a better partner than Him!

Now, look back at the Parable of The Bridesmaids, in Matthew 25, our KEY TEXT. The inference here is that we have to be watching, waiting and ready to go! How do we do that?

Through Prayer

This brings us to our first step in possessing the POISED state, of Bride-Mentality; we *must learn to be powerful in prayer!* Prayer can send ripples throughout the heavenlies. Prayer creates divine opportunities. To my point, in January of 2012, the Spirit of God prompted me to start getting up early to pray…to "*step it up, a notch!* "

Now, I confess that I had become irregular in prayer, prior to that time; prayer for me had become hit and miss and mostly miss. I had fallen off the prayer wagon and wasn't being diligent about a regular time each day, where I would seek the face of God. (Uhhhh, I know that's never happened to any of you.) So, I heeded that urgent prompting.

Prayer is the vehicle where God-Ideas are conceived. Our creative potential can be realized when we pray. He whispers to us, all sorts of wonderful things. In fact, it wasn't long after I obeyed His urgent prompting, that the God-idea for this book was born. **POISED, With Bride Mentality**, came straight from my prayer closet! (Super Like)

How about you? How's your prayer life working for ya?

You may already be a Powerhouse, or you may be like I was two years ago and could use a good slap on the behind, to get you back on track. Well, allow my book to do just that! In fact, I have prayed that it would. You know, God's got our number. We can act spiritual around people all we want but we're no greater than our own personal prayer life, friends. It's a truly humbling thought.

King David prayed this prayer in Psalms 27, *"Hear me as I pray, O Lord. Be merciful and answer me! My heart has heard you say, 'Come and talk with me'. And my heart responds, 'Lord, I am coming'."*

The Genesis of your turn-around, *the thing you need God to do in your life the most,* starts and ends with PRAYER and can I just say that we pay a HUGE price for compromise in this area? Consequently, one of the first things we give up, when we grieve the Spirit of God by ignoring Him in prayer, is *His still small voice.* The Spirit will **not compete** with our busy schedules. If we're too busy to pray then excuse me, but we're too busy. There are no Big **I's** and little **you's** in the Kingdom of God. We are *all* called to have intimacy in prayer with the Lover of our Soul...Our Bridegroom, Jesus.

The second thing we give up is fresh direction. So then, the flesh typically begins relying on **past** (or old), direction. It's a tell-tale sign that we're not praying. Other times human nature will even use what *someone else* got from God because we're not disciplining ourselves to do what it takes in prayer, to get *our own* God-Whispers.

Dear Reader, I don't want to rely on yesterday's words of direction or what somebody else heard God say to them. *I want fresh words from God's throne for myself.* Don't you? (I suspect you do) I want daily God-whispers in my life that only come from sitting at his feet in prayer and we can have that!

Getting alone with Him, in prayer is a type of marital courtship that He has created for His Church Bride. It's beautiful. The flesh cannot manufacture that and there is no replacement for it. And Oh! The blessings He bestows on those who love Him back. He will start moving in your life and the lives of those you care about, like you've never seen before, when you PRAY.

The Demoniac Boy and his Father (Mark 9:16-29)

Even the disciples of Jesus had to learn what happens when they tried to operate daily life, without the power of prayer. Let's look at this story:

Did you know that Jesus got frustrated too? He did!

Perhaps nothing frustrates Jesus more than His Church not using the spiritual authority He's given to us.

We see a frustrated Jesus in verse 19 –"You faithless people! How long must I be with you? How long must I put up with you? (You can almost hear the SIGH, in His voice) Bring the boy to me!" (The implication here is, "I guess I'll have to do it myself!")

(Well, Alrighty Then!) F-R-U-S-T-R-A-T-E-D! The boy's father tattled on the disciples…"I asked your disciples to cast out the evil spirit, but they couldn't do it." We see Jesus command the evil spirit and the boy is delivered immediately. Afterward, when Jesus was alone in the house with His disciples, they asked Him, "Why couldn't we cast out that evil spirit?" to which Jesus replied, "This kind can be cast out only by prayer".

*Only by Prayer? Yes, Only by Prayer. We've **GOT** to have a Prayer life!*

Let's quit talking about everything and start praying about everything.

"Drop the frown and just kneel down!"

Psalm 91:1 says it best, "They that dwell in the secret place of the most High, shall abide under the shadow of the Almighty." There is a covering of safety and protection from the storms of life, when we pray. It doesn't mean there won't be storms…it means we will have an insulator as we go through them. It's a place of Favor, up under His wings, up under His feathers, like a Mother bird with her chicks…dwelling there. Dwell means HABITATE. You can "live" in a perpetual state of prayer and still go about your daily life's work. No one will know it but you and God. We can pray with our heart and mind continually, in the Spirit. Withdraw yourself. Jesus did. He pulled away and got alone with God.

"And He withdrew into the desert and prayed." [7]

"El Shaddai", one of the Hebrew names for God means, "The many breasted one". Stay in the shadow of His protection, through prayer. Where do shadows fall? BEHIND. Stay behind, in His shadow. Follow God. Don't get out ahead of Him. These are the practical tactics that I'm teaching you, to give you power in your prayer life. My Guide will help you to list your special prayer needs and journal your prayers for each one of them. I recommend this tool, if you want to see more productivity in your life, in the area of prayer.

Chapter Two~

MY FATHER ~ MY CROWN

**"Quit praying the problem and
start praying the PROMISES!"**

*A*llow me to give a little more back story. I first learned the power of prayer as a teenage girl. As soon as I became a Christian, I found a scripture in Acts 16:31 (NLV), that became my mantra.

"Believe in the Lord Jesus, and you will be saved, along with everyone in your household."

Since I was the first Christian in my immediate family, I felt God had reached down to me and was raising me up, to reach them. I prayed from 1973–1988 for my alcoholic father to be saved. That is fifteen years! It took that long to see him delivered from demon spirits and come to Christ, not because God wasn't powerful enough to do it sooner but because He allows us to be free moral agents and to surrender to Him of our own will.

So, the whole time I was at Central Bible College in Springfield, Missouri as a student, I carried an intense prayer-burden for my father. His condition had rapidly deteriorated, after my parents' divorce and he had gone missing. He became a transient individual living from one half-way house to the next, sometimes homeless altogether, sleeping under street bridges, and eventually, winding up in a Detox or Psychiatric Unit of a hospital suffering from a nervous breakdown. I would hear other voices speak out of him, many times. Not the normal pleasant tones of my father's voice but low, growling voices that were hard to hear. He was driven to drink and tormented by memories of separation from his brothers and sisters, after the death of both parents and being sent to an orphanage to live. I KNEW that no one else was praying for him and that if I did not, he would die and go to HELL! So, I was assigned to pray for him. But it's kind of hard to pray for someone you can't stand and harbor resentment toward. (Get the picture?)

But still...God directed me to pray for him and that eventually gave way to **compassion.** *So, I would take pillow and blanket, nearly every night at* CBC and head toward the end of my Dorm Hall where the Prayer Room was located. There, I would pray, sleep a little, wake up and pray again through the night. I did that for four years. Honestly, It seemed the harder I prayed, the worse he got. The enemy was fighting. One evening, my Dad called my dorm phone, intoxicated and asking for money. I was always embarrassed by him. I prayed harder. I found the scripture in **Matthew 18:18 (NLV)** and it empowered me to pray more fervently, with authority. (I talk about spiritual authority in more detail in PART SIX- on DOMINION).

Jesus is teaching here, *"I tell you the truth, whatever you forbid (or bind) on earth, will be forbidden (or bound) in heaven, and whatever you permit (loose) on earth will be permitted (loosed) in heaven."*

I would bind the evil spirits that were tormenting him, in Jesus name and command them to loose my father and let him go. Then I would pray that the ministering angels of God through the power of the Holy Spirit would draw him to Jesus, that he would find no rest until he came to Christ. I also forbid Satan from killing him before he could get saved. I did this daily. *You can use this same scripture and prayer for your loved ones.*

One of the greatest joys for any father is the proud moment he has the privilege of walking his daughter down the aisle on her wedding day. However, unable to walk his daughter down the aisle on wedding day, my own father sat on the front row of the church, as an observer...with the three-hour pass, previously issued from the psychiatric hospital, hidden in his front pocket. He was known by every Detox Unit and Psychiatric Ward in Jacksonville, Florida at the time and would suffer an enduring cycle of binge drinking, nervous breakdown and Rehab.

I prayed harder. My heart broke for him. But I would get so frustrated... I would give up! Then, feeling convicted by the Holy Spirit, I would repent and get back on the prayer wagon. I would pray, get frustrated, quit, then feel convicted by the Holy Spirit and repent and *get back on the wagon*... **for fifteen years.**

By 1988, Mark and I were married, busy in full-time ministry and had a two year old son, named Luke. I had to keep Luke away from "Peepa Larry" much of the time, to protect him from exposure and influence of evil spirits residing in my father. It was sad but necessary. Luke prayed every night for his "Peepa Larry" to be saved. I love children's faith. He would pray so sweetly for his Grandpa.

We were pastoring a church in Illinois at the time and lived next door in a parsonage. A call came late one night and Mark answered the phone. It was my dad. He sounded intoxicated, as usual. Mark was used to this too, in the seven years we'd been married and so we had an agreement that I would always "handle it". I would use the phone as a point of contact and pray quietly in the Spirit over him, as he rambled on, at the other end. It was my only contact with him and I made the most of it. I would pray God's delivering power to break the satanic hold and generational curse on him, in Jesus name and eventually, Dad would just hang up.

But this night, in 1988...this Sunday night, in 1988... something was different! He was not his usual intoxicated self. He sounded drunk but his speech was not slurred. I listened more closely. He was relating a story. An amazing story!

Dad had been walking along University Boulevard that Sunday evening in Jacksonville, Florida, drinking heavily and looking for more, when he heard it.

The Sound of Music coming from a Jewish Synagogue!

The Synagogue was right next door to a BINGO hall, where he played weekly. *My dad LOVED the game of Bingo!* (Wink) He stumbled closer. "Yes", he mused to himself. "There's definitely music coming from that building and where there is music...there is probably a party!" he concluded. So he entered. What he did not know, was that this was a Spirit-filled church that was temporarily renting the facility on Sundays, from the Jewish Synagogue, while their new church was being built! And something else that he did not know, this was **my home church** and my home-town Pastor that helped put me through Bible College at CBC! (Big Smile)

"Welcome", gushed the ushers who met my intoxicated father at the entrance. "We've been expecting you"! And they had, this church prayed frequently that God would send in the lost, hurting and the broken to their church.

So, over the parsonage phone, Dad related to me how the men took him to the church kitchen and sat him down. They offered him a cup of coffee and a little sandwich. They washed his face and combed his hair. He told me how kind they were to him. They ministered to him, the love of Christ and after about fifteen minutes, they asked him if he would like to join them and go into the service. They told him they had a special reserved seat just for him. His reply? "Ok, I've got a daughter that believes like you do" and so they went into the service. They took him to a seat on the front row and stayed with him. The message was just getting started by the Pastor, Paul D. Zink. Dad listened quietly. The Holy Spirit was already helping him to become sober in that short time and began moving on his heart. He felt the drawing power of God, he said. At the altar call, Dad responded to the message and went forward of his own free will. He fell on the carpet with a "thud", unable to stand under the delivering power of God. Through the powerful prayers of the church leadership, who laid hands on him, he was delivered of every one of those demon spirits and prayed the "Sinner's prayer" with them! He didn't know it was my home church and they didn't know he was **Susie McGrath's** father **but God did**.

Fifteen years of carpet-eating prayer had culminated into **dramatic** answer to prayer, with some of the most unique, God-like "co-incidences", that I've EVER heard of. (Happy Dance!) Now, he was calling our parsonage in Illinois on that Sunday night, to tell us the wonderful news.

Was it real? Did it last? Here's the answer.

From that day forward, he never got drunk again. He began to rehabilitate into a functioning individual, one in his right mind. He got an apartment and he lived in that same little, one bedroom apartment for twenty years. He lived there from 1990–2011, when he died. This was something he'd never been able to do before. When we were cleaning out his things, the apartment manager told me that he was one of the most pleasant, well-liked and faithful tenants they'd ever had and with tears in her eyes, talked about how much they would miss "Mr. Larry".

Trying to make up for lost time, dad never missed a birthday or Christmas after that. And my son and daughter can attest to the fact that he would call and send sweet notes with a little money or gift inside, for all their important days, till the day he died. All evidences of a life-transformed by the supreme power of God.

Dad and I had many conversations about heaven after his conversion but he never seemed to get over the guilt of being a "bad father". He struggled to gain assurance that God had really forgiven him. We prayed on many occasions together for God to give him peace and healing from the past and that he would forgive himself. It was amazing to see the change...he wasn't perfect but changed and when he died in August, 2011, at the age of seventy-seven; Mark and I were there to hold his hand and to pray with him. I sang these words over him in his hospital bed, *as this time,* **he was "Ushered" one final time,** into the presence of the King of Kings and Lord of Lords. However this time, by a very different set of ushers...the angels of heaven!

"Peace, Peace, Wonderful Peace.
Coming down, from the Father above.
Sweep over my spirit, forever I Pray,
In fathomless billows of Love."

Yes, my Father is my greatest prayer trophy, my crown. And one day, I will give my crown to Jesus and Dad will be right there with me, when I do.

"Therefore, my dear brothers and sisters, stay true to the Lord. I love you and long to see you, dear friends, for you are my joy and the crown I receive for my work." Philippians 4:1 (NIV)

Chapter Three~

PITIFUL OR POWERFUL~
WHICH WAY DO YOU PRAY?

"Drop the Frown and just Kneel Down".

Bride Mentality Prays!

Bride Mentality **IS** prayer mentality. Every day we awaken, we are on assignment. It's not about us. It's about those around us—It's called **Compassion.**

- Want more power in your life? Start praying.
- Want more direction in your life? Start praying.
- Want more answers in your life? (well, you get the picture)

7 Hindrances to Prayer:

1) *We don't know WHO we are in God.*
2) *We question the value of prayer.*
3) *We don't make time for prayer.*
4) *We pray the problem and not the promises!*
5) *We put prayer at the mercies of our feelings.*
6) *We're lazy and selfish.*
7) *We don't believe He'll answer us.*

7 Reasons for Unanswered Prayer:

1) *We quit!*
2) *Sin in our heart*
3) *Possessing Wrong motives*
4) *Lack of Faith*
5) *Mistreatment of Family Members*

6) *The lack of Generosity*

7) *Having an Unforgiving Spirit*

7 Reasons for Answered Prayer:

1) Not Quitting (get back on the wagon!)

2) Pray to the Father.

3) Pray in the name of Jesus.

4) We pray with full understanding of our rights and privileges.

5) We pray the Word of God.

6) We make a definite time and place for prayer.

7) We pray in faith, doubting nothing.

Why do we pray?

- God Commands it (Luke 18:1)
- It moves the hand of God (Matthew 11:28)
- Prayer blesses others (1 Timothy 2:11)
- Leadership of the World (2 Timothy 1:4)
- Pray for the Lost, for the Nations of the World (Psalm 2:8)

What is it that you're believing God for right now? What *unanswered prayer* is hanging over your life like a big, black cloud?

Can I challenge your Bride Mentality here? **P-R-A-Y!** "Drop the frown and just kneel down."

"You Da Bride...Be Da Bride!"

Take the spiritual authority that Jesus gave to all of us and get back down on your knees with it. Winners never quit and quitters never win. If I had to do life all over again, I really don't think I'd change much, even the hard things. Because having to pray for hard things, puts steel in your spine. It teaches perseverance. It puts grit in your soul, like the old negro-spiritual says.

"You don't know like I know; what the Lord has done for me!"

Prayer teaches us that prayer works. We focus on the miracle we need, God focuses on the benefit of waiting. Muscles are strengthened through exercise and prayer strengthens the spiritual heart. Prayer is exercise! It is Labor! The more we pray, the more we can pray. **James 5:16 (NIV)** says:

"The effectual fervent prayer of a righteous man or woman, avails much. "

But sometimes we don't pray because we're afraid it will cost us something. We're afraid God will ask us to DO something.

THE MAN AND THE VAN

I am reminded of a man named Sam (not his real name). He was in one of our pastorates many years ago. Sam would go to prayer and each time he did, the Spirit of God would direct him to go buy a van for the church and use it to pick up children and teens for the mid-week service. He had the ability financially, to buy the van but he was resisting and he was *MISERABLE*. Sam began having sleeping problems. He would toss and turn all night thinking about all those children and teenagers.

Finally, he gave in and came to talk with my husband, the Pastor and told him the story. They prayed together and he finally gave in to the strong urgency of the Spirit. Within that year, twelve to fifteen boys began riding the new van on Wednesday night, to our youth service. They were all from Methodist families, whose church did not have a mid-week service. After some weeks, the families of all those boys began visiting our church on Sunday nights, since the Methodist Church only met on Sunday morning.

I'm happy to say that we saw dozens of those students and their parents filled with the Holy Spirit that year and a Revival of Spiritual Renewal began in that county, all because one man obeyed what God was telling him, while on his knees in prayer. Prayer may cost you something but the reward **always** outweighs the sacrifice!

~When we Pray, God will Say and then we must Obey!

Chapter Four~

THE MIRACLE OF THE MONEY CLIP

"We focus on the Miracle, God sees the value of Waiting."

*Y*ou gotta love Disney World! Mickey Mouse, the Magic Kingdom…it brings out the kid in all of us! We were headed there, that bright December day, in 1995. Our daughter, Lyndi was just six months old. It would be her first trip to see "Minnie". Also along for the fun, were my Mother and Father-in-law, Bill and Wanda Purkey. As we headed south in our mini-van, excitement was HIGH. We just had to stop in Louisiana to minister in a church, on the way down and our vacay would officially commence. Florida here we come! Deciding to go "All Cash, No Credit", on the trip, I cautioned my husband to keep his mind on his money at all times. (Insert wink here)

We concluded our Sunday morning service that day and stopped at the local gas station for a quick fill-up, before getting on the road. When he went to pay for the gas, he couldn't find his money clip. We all searched. Perhaps it fell on the ground, by the pumps? No. Maybe it was under the driver's seat of the car, on the floor board? Still nothing. We were trying not to panic but the atmosphere was *TENSE.* I did what any self-respecting wife would do and resorted to blame and accusation. (Ah, Hem), "Didn't we discuss how you needed to keep your mind on your money, *DEAR?" I quipped.* I could hear my mother-in-law, in the back seat, praying. We all took a deep breath. Dad Purkey paid for the gas, until we could locate our money. Wanda prayed that God's angels would bring the money back to us. So, with heavy hearts, we proceeded in the direction of our destination and drove off.

It was a torturously long day ahead of us. Seven hundred and eight miles from Monroe, Louisiana to Jacksonville, Florida and the ten and a half hour trip was exacerbated by the growing concern over the missing money clip. We tried not to talk about it and trusted the Lord. After all, we had two children in the car and this was their special Christmas vacation to Disney World. We sang songs, we licked candy canes, we listened to Elvis' Blue Christmas... and we believed God for a miracle. (What a Combo)

We stopped along the way only to gas up the car and eat meals, finally arriving at my mother's house after dark that night. Exhausted, we unloaded only what we **had** to have for the night and headed to our beds, with the sinking realization, that the trip to Disney World would probably be off now.

The next morning, the December frost had settled over everything in the north Florida area. There in the Sunshine State, as the first sun hit the grass, it made the water crystals sparkle like diamonds. Mark and Luke, who was nine years old at the time, sleepily headed outside, to begin unloading a few more things from the car. As Luke approached the driver's side door, he saw it! There on the wet grass lay several $100 bills! Gasping, he called for his dad. Together, they stooped down picking up the damp bills. They couldn't believe their eyes. "What in the world?" Mark said out loud. Opening the door of the car, a few more $100 bills fell out. "Dad, LOOK!" Luke exclaimed. The two, now down on their hands and knees began picking up the additional money from the soggy grass. Mark re-searched the floor board and under seat area but it revealed nothing new. However, bending lower, he further inspected the door storage area, even feeling along the bottom of the door itself, with his hand. "THERE! What was that?" he thought to himself. It was the Missing money clip!

The magnetic clip was firmly "stuck" to the very bottom of the metal driver's-side door, where it had fallen from his lap, ten and a half hours previously; after Mark got out of the car to fill up with gas in Monroe! A quick recount of the bills revealed the original sum. Not a single dollar had been lost! Why hadn't any of the bills or the clip itself, fallen out before, on the numerous times that door was opened and closed for stops along the way? Why did they fall out only when we reached our destination, of my mother's house? Why did it finally fall out at all and when it did, why had it fallen out in the early morning, when there was little wind and no passers-by?

Because God Hears and Answers Specific Prayer.

That was the most memorable vacation our family ever had. Disney World was never more fun…paid in full, by the angels of God who held that money clip in place for over seven hundred miles and across three states. I learned that Christmas, to *NEVER* underestimate the power of prayer **or** a praying Grandma!

Chapter Five ~

FASTING SESSION 101 AND MY DAILY PRAYER COVERING

"Some kind only come out by

prayer and fasting." Jesus

Fasting Session 101

Why Fast?

The essence of the spiritual fast: is to strengthen true repentance and to offer true humility. Such spiritual fasting helps to remind us of our unworthiness as sinners, and it leads us—sometimes in a sense of desperation, to ask for God's tender mercies and forgiveness. Humility and self-denial are two sides of the same spiritual coin. In order to deny ourselves at our own expense and for the benefit of others, we must have humility in our hearts. (Matthew 16:24)

Built into this ultimate denial of "taking up the cross", is the denial inherent in fasting unto the Lord. Fasting denies that which legitimately belongs to us: the joy of eating. By fasting unto the Lord, we answer His call to deny ourselves for the sake of the cross. Whether practiced by a corporate body in a proclaimed fast or by one person in an individual fast, the fast of repentance and humility is the true spiritual fast. The early mosaic expression for fasting is "to afflict, bow or humble the soul" by restraining the earthly appetites that have their seat in the soul.

God wants His people to feast and fast. We can be sensitive about the timing of both. (Ecclesiastes 3:1) In many places throughout Scripture, the word **mourning** can be used interchangeably with fasting. For instance, when Daniel referred to his twenty-one day fast, he said, "In those days, I Daniel was mourning three full weeks". (Daniel 10:2)

The New Testament also supports this truth. When the disciples of John the Baptist asked why they fasted and Jesus' disciples didn't, Jesus replied,

"Do wedding guests mourn while celebrating with the groom? Of course not but someday the groom will be taken away from them, and then they will fast." [8]

Jesus used the word mourn, to indicate that while He was with His disciples—while the bridegroom was present—it wasn't the proper time to fast. Why? Because Jesus' time on earth marked a time of joyous celebration! He also said that His disciples would mourn after the Bridegroom was taken away but because of the expectation of His second coming, fasting would be practiced with new meaning. Mourning would be intermixed with joy.

"To all who mourn in Israel, He will give a crown of beauty for ashes, a joyous blessing instead of mourning, festive praise instead of despair, In their righteousness, they will be like great oaks that the Lord has planted for His own glory." [9]

The New Testament Fast, therefore, was something new and distinct from previous practices. The Christian basis for fasting–the sacrifices of Jesus and the inner confidence, trust and joy motivated by His love, make fasting an entirely different experience than the traditional Judaic fast. God has set His children free from sin! With that freedom, we also enjoy our glorious salvation, which gives us a new and stronger basis for fasting unto the Lord. Mourning was used synonymously with fasting because it characterized how Christians wait for the second coming of Christ. (Matthew 5:4) probably included fasting.

"God blesses those who mourn, for they will be comforted."

Examples of instances of lamentation or deep sadness where the ancients undoubtedly fasted include:
- Defeat in battle. (Judges 20:25-26)
- For sad tidings (Nehemiah 1:4)
- The onset of plagues (Joel 1:2-4;13-14; 2:12-15)

- For the threat of disaster (2 Chronicles 20:1-3; Esther 4:3; 9:30-31)

Fasting provides the opportunity to show personal humility before God and to plead for mercy—**not to force his hand!** So, why is it so important to deny myself? Think of the spoiled child who always gets his/her own way. No one can stand to be around selfish people who have no depth, no integrity and no strength of character. Practicing self-denial builds character. Our personal acts of self-denial encourage us to seek the Lord more fully and to become more Christ-like.

> "For if you live by its dictates, you will die but if through the power of the Spirit you put to death the deeds of your sinful nature, you will live." [10]

The way to glorify God and to become more like Christ is through the narrow road of self-denial and what more demanding way to deny self, than to fast unto the Lord?

How to Fast?

Anoint with oil—Jesus rebuked the false piety of the Pharisees, but He also instructed His disciples how to fast.

"But when you fast, comb your hair and wash your face. Then no one will notice that you are fasting, except your Father, who knows what you do in private. And your Father, who sees everything, will reward you." [11]

Like the Pharisees, the ancients didn't use oil during a fast. Since oil represented joy, it was commonly used to anoint kings, priests and prophets. The Pharisees strictly forbade washing the face and anointing the head during a fast. Jesus changed the anointing customs once and for all. Washing the face and anointing the head with oil became the new way to fast. Christ's disciples didn't need to smear ashes on their faces. Jesus told them to wash their faces. Isaiah 61:3, (cited previously).

Because emotional balance contributes to effective-ness of fasting, it's advisable to prayerfully consider **when** one should fast. If your faith in fasting is strong, times of emotional turmoil may be the best time to rest in the Lord and fast. However, if the emotional turmoil is too upsetting, you should probably continue eating regular meals until balance is restored.

The following times bring additional stress:

- The trauma of separation or divorce
- The loss of a loved one
- Pregnancy and nursing after giving birth
- Stressful situations that cause anger, extreme anxiety or any other intense emotional strain.

Exceptions of course, do occur. You need to be sensitive to the Holy Spirit to discern His will. Even though you may be suffering grief, stress, or intense emotional strain, God may still lead you to fast.

How will you know? Ask yourself the following questions:

- Have I received a special message from God to fast?
- Have I reached a place of spiritual desperation and temporarily lost the desire for food?
- Have I decided to fast for a specific health problem?

By now you should be gaining confidence in this neglected discipline. If you understand the following three points, you can conquer the fear of fasting:

1) Fasting does not harm our bodies. Moderate, sensibly conducted fasting actually benefits the body.

2) Most of us can fast many days, even several weeks, on the stored reserves in the body.

3) The body always signals when it's through fasting and requires food.

Before you fast, prepare yourself spiritually.

Meditate on scriptures. (Galatians 5:16-17; 1Peter 5:8; Ephesians 6:11; Romans 6:12-13; Psalms 139:14; 1John 3:22; 1 Corinthians 10:31; Proverbs 4:20-22).

Before you fast, also prepare yourself physically.

Because many people experience a great drop in their blood sugar when they forsake their usual high-fat, high-sugar diets, you may want to wean yourself from these foods a day or two before you fast. If you're a heavy coffee or tea drinker, gradually cut the caffeine from your diet. Fasters commonly experience headaches, a withdraw symptom of forgoing their usual large amounts of caffeine and sugar. Eliminating these foods before the fast will decrease the likelihood of your suffering with headaches, dizziness and cravings.

What is a total fast?

The total fast is conducted by abstaining from both food and water. Some people know this as "the Esther fast". (Esther 4:16)

Moses participated in a total fast right before he came down from the mountain carrying the Ten Commandments. The bible says that he fasted a total of 80 days taking no food or drink. This was a supernatural fast because no human can live without water that long. (Deuteronomy 9:9; 18 & 25-29; 10:10) *Most experts on fasting agree, that a total fast (no food or water) should not last more than three days.* Even three days is considered risky and is definitely not recommended. Do this only when you know you have received definite and specific instruction from God.

What is an Absolute Fast?

The absolute fast is a fast in which one abstains from all solid and liquid foods. **This fast permits only water.** During the total and absolute fasts, the sensation of hunger is absent. Because the body actually feeds on its own reserves, one does not experience hunger. Fasters usually understand this truth; *"Appetite is a mental desire; hunger is a bodily need."* Since the bodily needs are being met while the body feeds on its available reserves, hunger is absent while fasting. Appetite may be present, but that is not true hunger. Most theologians agree that Jesus undertook a forty day absolute fast rather than a total fast, for two reasons.

1) The bible does not specify that He took neither food nor water, as it does in the cases of Moses, Esther, Ezra and others.

2) Matthew and Luke both said that Christ was hungry after His forty-day fast (see Matthew 4:2 and Luke 4:2); Scripture does not say that He was thirsty. Since thirst is a much stronger and more urgent desire than hunger, if Jesus had been without water while fasting, He surely would have wanted it before food.

Most people can undergo their own absolute fast with nothing but fabulous results. It is recommended however, that you don't enter into an absolute fast for more than 5 days unless you are an experienced faster or under professional supervision. A few people, however (you may be one of them), may need consultation and responsible supervision due to special medications you are taking.

As a general rule you should stop all medications before an absolute or total fast. If you are one who cannot go off medicines without negative repercussions, than a partial fast would be a better choice.

What is a Partial Fast?

The partial fast means abstinence from certain, select foods and drinks but not complete abstinence from all foods and drinks. For instance, Daniel abstained from bread, meat and wine for twenty-one days. (Daniel 10:3) This means that everyone who refrains from eating a particular food is on a partial fast. We do not usually consider vegetarians to be on a partial fast just because they are abstaining from meat. They are practicing a vegetarian eating style...not fasting.

It is recommended, generally speaking, for most individuals to begin their fasting experience with the partial fast. (Especially if strong medications are involved). Also, this is a fast that allows a person to maintain strength so that they can continue their daily routine.

- **The juice diet** is the most popular form of the partial fast. Perhaps the most important items to remember when on the juice diet are to drink fresh juices, consume them slowly, and take no more than five glasses daily.

The partial fast taken for spiritual reasons should eliminate some favorite foods–those we regularly eat and especially enjoy, crave and overeat. Scripture tells us that Daniel ate **"no pleasant food"**. (Daniel 10:3) Daniel's diet was a partial fast (aka, The Daniel Fast). He ate only certain grains, legumes and vegetables. According to Scripture, Daniel's diet permitted no animal products such as meat, milk and eggs.

What is the difference between Daniel's partial fast and the Genesis 1:29 Diet?

Although both are vegan, the Genesis 1:29 diet requires no cooking. The person on this diet eats fruits and vegetables in their raw, uncooked state.

One may use the partial fast to humble himself before God. It can be used as a sacrifice by denying yourself something you like very much. One Jewish man fasted desserts because he dearly loved them. **Partial fasts should not include foods that we eat and enjoy regularly. It is also urged, that people who are fasting abstain from television, newspaper, social media and**

hobbies. While not technically part of a fast, forgoing the media and other indulgences parallels the discipline needed for the partial fast. This discipline frees time for prayer and Scripture study and helps to remind us that fasting is more than merely going without food.

If the idea of going without any food is not comfortable to you, then the partial fast is a good way to begin acquiring your fasting experience. You do not suffer the physical, emotional and spiritual shock of having all your food yanked away from you. After undertaking the partial fast of your choice a few times, you'll learn that you don't need to fear undertaking the absolute fast for a day.

Once you're convinced of the benefits of fasting, you should decide the proper time to undertake a fast. A short fast of one to three days can be taken virtually anytime. Fasting from Friday evening to Monday morning would give you the entire weekend to rest and spend time reading Scripture. Another ideal time is during vacations from work. You can plan an extended period of several days to fast.

Breaking a Fast-

You can choose one of two following ways to come off a Total or Absolute Fast:

1) You may take juices. On the first day, take four ounces of fresh juice every two hours starting at 8:00 a.m. and ending at 6:00 p.m. On the next two or three days, take 8-10 ounces of freshly made juice for breakfast, lunch and dinner.

2) You may take fruit. On the first day, take an eight ounce serving of fresh fruit every 2 hours, starting at 8:00 am, and ending at 6:00 p.m. On the next two or three days, take eight ounces of fruit for breakfast, lunch and dinner.

Be sure to eat slowly and chew your food well.

Jesus received rich rewards for overcoming temptation during His fasts. Although He had performed no miracle before His fast, He immediately stepped into His new ministry, afterward. **We too, can expect supernatural strength, answers to prayer and even miracles from prayer coupled with fasting unto the Lord!**

God Bless you as you Go to the next level with the Lord! [12]

DAILY PRAYER COVERING

Daily, you can pray this out-loud,

in the form of a declaration:

Father, I come to you in the Name of Jesus, my Savior.

I come boldly upon your throne of grace, asking for mercy and grace to help me in time of need, in accordance with (Hebrew 4:16).

I ask that you would bless me in all areas of my life, today.

I pray that you would bless the work of my hands and help me to be fruitful.

I pray for FAVOR in the marketplace today. Thank you for your provision in my life. Thank you for Favor and Increase today, in Jesus Name!

I take authority over every weapon that would be formed against me, or my loved ones, that it would Not Prosper. In Jesus mighty name, I bind Poverty, Lack, Sickness, Disease and Infirmity. Take it from our midst. (Call this covering over your spouse, children, grandchildren, by inserting their names).

Father, I lean NOT on my own understanding, education, talents, abilities, appearance or gifts today but wholly upon your Spirit!

I Lean On You! In all my ways, I acknowledge my need of you today, Lord. Please direct my path and use me today for your glory and I will give you all the praise (credit), in Jesus Name. Amen

~~~BRIDE MENTALITY~~~
PART TWO

P.

O. is for Obedience

I.

S.

E.

D.

Chapter Six ~

THE PIE LADY

**"As faith is the principle by which we obtain life,
so obedience is the principle by
which that life is lived out."**

Watchman Nee

*A*t the time of this writing, my husband and I have accomplished sixty missionary journeys throughout the world. We will complete three more, God willing, by the time this book is published. Traveling to approximately twenty-two nations of the world has been an extreme privilege and we have a two-fold purpose in doing so:

1) To win the lost to Jesus Christ

2) To build up the existing Church of our Lord

Twenty-two of those sixty missionary journeys have been to Rome, Italy alone. In Rome, we have conducted nightly crusades, witnessed healings in the shadow of the Vatican and walked in Paul's footsteps along the Appian Way and in the underground Catacombs. At the great Coliseum, constructed in 80 A.D., which was the site of countless Christians who were martyred for their faith, we have held prayer meetings on that holy ground, with our teams. We have taken scores of teams. One of our favorite places in Rome, is Paul's prison. It's just steps away from the great Coliseum and the site where the Apostle Paul wrote much of the New Testament while being chained in an damp, dark, underground hole. How I Love Roma!

The bible says, "Work hard to show the results of your salvation, obeying God with deep reverence and fear. For

God is working in you, giving you the desire and the power to do what pleases Him."[13]

God gives us the desire to DO what He's asking of us! How cool is that?

- What has God placed in your heart to do for Him, to make the world a better place?
- Do you have a dream? He will equip you when He leads you...Just ask him–**then obey.**

Pray and Obey...Obedience IS worship, friends. He has **given** His promise for every generation past, present and future and It **applies t**o every generation, past, present and future. As I mentioned in my back story, I come from a family with three generations of "Alcoholics". Each generation has become more dysfunctional and deteriorated. That's what we refer to as a "Generational Curse". My Grandfather was an alcoholic, my father was an alcoholic and I have siblings who have the disease. I should have the disease as well. Why am I different?

I broke the curse through OBEDIENCE.

Dear Reader, one drop of the blood of Jesus, is enough to break every inherited tendency toward evil!

When I had an opportunity to invite Jesus Christ into my heart and made Him the Lord of my life, **I chose to be blessed.** Now, I and my children walk in a Generational **Blessing**! Hallelujah! But each Generation has its own responsibilities to choose God and it's a sobering thought to realize that Christianity is only one generation away from "Extinction".

"Now listen! Today I am giving you a choice between life and death, between prosperity and disaster. For I command you this day to love the Lord your God and to keep His commands, decrees and regulations by walking in His ways. If you do this, you will live and multiply and the Lord your God will bless you and the land you are about to enter and occupy." [14]

Yes, I chose to allow God to direct my path and more importantly, I followed. I find that it's not that difficult. **Just choose life!** (Talk about a no-brainer!)

In the past thirty years, our main purpose has been to share what God has done for us, in the hopes that others bound in sin, trapped in a bad home life or perhaps even generations of dysfunction, like I was in, could have hope and happiness. We've shared this message all over the world and I'm happy to report we've seen thousands of people give their hearts to Christ.

BRIDE MENTALITY OBEYS~

The Church-Bride receives God's outstretched scepter of Favor because she has willingly followed His just commands. That's what Blessed means–*FAVOR*. Everyone **wants** God's Favor but not everyone wants to **do what it takes** to **receive** God's Favor. When our bridegroom, Jesus returns for His Church-Bride, she will go with Him into heaven, to the Marriage Supper of the Lamb. (Matthew 25:10) We call it the Rapture of the Church and this is where our true union with our Lord will be consummated. We will finally see Him face to face.

The Secret of the Blessed Life is to simply love God **enough** to obey his Word.

"If you love me, obey my commandments. And I will ask the Father and He will give you another Advocate, who will never leave you. He is the Holy Spirit who leads you into all truth. Those who accept my commands and obey them are the ones who love me. And because they love me, my Father will love them. And I will love them and reveal myself to each of them." [15]

THE PIE LADY~

Several years ago, when week-long Revivals were more prevalent, my husband was holding a meeting in Wichita, Kansas. On the Sunday morning, that he began his meeting, he preached a message on Obedience and the altars were full at the end of his sermon. However, he noticed a well-dressed, elderly lady sitting all alone toward the back of the auditorium and felt directed to go to her.

"The Lord wants to use you. What talents or gifts do you possess?" he inquired. "I don't have any", she quickly said in a forlorn voice. "Oh Come On", he shot back. "Everyone can do *something*. What are you good at?" he countered. Their eyes locked for a moment. Reluctantly she said, "Well…at one time, people around here said I made the best pies in the county." She went on to say that a local restaurant even bought her pies each week for their local menu. "Well then, the Lord says it's time to Pre-heat Your Oven Again!" my husband announced to her. "What? I don't do **that** anymore!" she retorted. "Precisely, and **that** is your problem! You've become withdrawn and alone and *it's All about YOU* but The Lord is saying to you today, it's time to get off your Pity Pot and pre-heat your oven again!

Starting this week, bake one pie a week and find someone else who is just as alone and unhappy and depressed as you are and take that pie to them!" He continued, as her eyes locked in on him like laser beams. "I'll be back in one year, your Pastor has already rescheduled with me and when I do, I'll check on how things are going with you, Deal?" "Deal." she hesitantly whispered.

One year later, my husband returned to that church for their annual Spiritual- Emphasis Week. As he walked out onto the platform that Sunday morning, he surveyed the crowd. The church was full but he was looking for one little lady, in particular. There she was, this time on the second row from the front and much to his surprise, she had an entire row packed with little white-haired women. They were fired up and ready to worship! Some of them had tambourines and they all sang fervently, praising God with up-lifted hands and hearts. When there was opportunity to greet one- another, Mark made a bee-line to "Sister Pie". (Insert wink here)

"What has happened to you?" he questioned excitedly, with a big smile on his face. "Well Preacher, I did exactly what the Lord told me", she announced proudly. "I took a pie a week to someone else as lonely as me and I led every one of these ladies to the Lord!" Then, she began to introduce each lady by name in this manner:

"Here's Ethel, she was coconut cream. There's Helen, she was dutch apple, Bertha here, was blueberry and Shirley and Martha were both lemon-meringue. And way down there is Margie and I got her with French silk! Etc. (Yes, I kid you not).

What is it that you need the Lord to do for you today?

Your answer may be just one pie away, so-to-speak. Think about your gifts and talents. What are YOU good at? Sow something good, into someone else's life as a seed offering to the Lord and watch Him work! *Pray this prayer as you do:*

"Lord, I plant this seed into someone else's life and I pray for my harvest, in Jesus name. Amen"

Can I just say for the record that many times in our lives, we get fixated on "Me, My, Mine"? That path leads to a very narrow place. It's a selfish place and it will suffocate you. We must let go of our own demanding desires and yield ourselves to the service of the Lord. The things He asks of each of us may be as different as the individual talents and gifts that we possess but just like the Pie Lady, they will be requests that require our Obedience. To obey is to find fulfillment and in the process of obeying, somewhere along the way, we find out that *our own needs were met!*

> *But Samuel the prophet replied, "What is more pleasing to the Lord; your burnt offerings and sacrifices or your obedience to His voice? Listen! Obedience is better than sacrifice and submission is better than offerings..."* [16]

FOUNDATIONS~

The foundations of our lives are as important as the foundation of a physical dwelling. Jesus says hearing and following His biblical instruction is essentially "the foundation of a Blessed Life".

> "So why do you keep calling me 'Lord, Lord' when you don't do what I say? I will show you what it is like when someone comes to me, listens to my teaching and then follows it. It is like a person building a house that digs deep and lays the foundation on solid rock. When the flood waters rise and break against the house, it stands firm because it is well

built but anyone who hears and doesn't *obey* is like a person who builds a house without a foundation. When the floods sweep down upon that house, it will collapse into a heap of ruins." [17]

When we were building our home a few years ago, the builder came to us and said "the soil in your area is a sandy/clay mix. I recommend that we increase your concrete foundation from twelve inches to eighteen inch for added strength". We discussed the significant increase in the cost and whether or not we wanted to start this huge project off, by going over budget on one of the first line-items. However, we both agreed that if you're going to skimp...don't skimp on your foundation...especially in our "tornado-alley" town of, Mustang, Oklahoma where we live. (Duh!)

This is exactly what Jesus was referring to in Luke the sixth chapter. Listening and following God's instructions through His Word is like building your life on Solid Rock! *Obedience is like Hazard Insurance!*

Chapter Seven~

CAN GOD HOLD A GRUDGE? FROM INTRODUCTION TO "I DO"~SHOULDN'T TAKE 40 YEARS

"Certain thicknesses require a drill-bit."

Can God Hold A Grudge?

"Don't harden your hearts as Israel did at Meribah, as they did at Massah in the wilderness. For there your ancestors tried my patience, even though they saw everything I did. For forty years I was angry with them, and I said, 'they are a people whose hearts turn away from me. They refuse to do what I tell them', so in my anger I took an oath: 'They will never enter my place of rest'." [18]

*U*h...Hello? I think that might be defined as a *righteous grudge*!

Bride-Mentality doesn't take "forever" (forty years), from "the introduction to the "I DO". In other words, acceptance and commitment follows in a timely manner. After all, He IS the Lover of our Soul. But this was not so with the Israelites crossing the hot, dry deserts of Egypt. You would think, after witnessing the hand of God parting the Red Sea right down the middle, they would have been convinced to follow and obey His lead. But they weren't. They griped and complained and had ungrateful spirits **in spite** of God providing everything they needed. Why, He even dropped bread from the sky every day and supernaturally preserved the sandals on their feet, so they wouldn't have to go to TARGET! (Ah, Hem) Were they thankful?

Not so much.

They murmured against their Pastor, Moses and plotted how they were going to "split the church".

And God got **very** angry with them. What happens when God gets ANGRY with His children?

It's about Circles.

He sends us wandering around in circles. And we all know you can't get very far going around in circles. But it **does** tend to give one **more time to think**... and that's just what happened to the Israelites in the desert. They circled and circled and circled and griped and murmured and complained. So God just said, "Take Another Lap!" And they never "got it"...for forty long years. However, after that time, it dawned on them that it might be better to just **OBEY**! (There's a thought)

And so it is.

We have a humorous saying in our family regarding "*IGNORANCE*". It goes like this:

"Certain thicknesses require a drill-bit."

There may have been one used with the Israelites in the desert but God **invented** the second chance. Did you know that? (*Well, er, uh, He actually invented EVERYTHING, but back to my point*). When we confess our sins, we invite God to wipe out the record of our past mistakes and rebellions. Then, we have a brand new opportunity to obey and live. The sins and mistakes of the past, trip us up, burden us down and hinder our success. But ah…confession is good for the Soul and paves the way for God to work within us, helping us to live by His power, through the Holy Spirit.

"People who conceal their sins will not prosper but if they confess and turn from them, they will receive mercy." [19]

- How about you? Does it seem that God isn't answering a prayer you're praying? Do you feel like you're trapped inside a Circle, wondering through a spiritual desert? Maybe you're just not seeing "The Blessing" in your life, like you see other's have.
- Could it be you've been disobedient in an area of your life? Maybe you haven't followed through on His instructions or finished strong with your whole

heart on something He's told you to do...like unforgiveness, for example? It was hard for me to forgive my father but God wouldn't bless me until I DID. Not just sins of **COMMISSION** but sins of **OMISSION**. Search your Heart.

You can't fool God, you know. God **cannot** and **will not** bless disobedience. It goes against His Word. What I'm speaking to you may even go against popular, tickle-your-ears preaching from feel-good-only churches. So be it. If you're feeling like this may be the reason for your dry season, pray this prayer with me right now:

"Father, I come to you in the name of Jesus. I'm discouraged and confused. It seems like every time I pray, my prayers just bounce off of the ceiling. I know you hear everything and know everything. I also know that you are a Holy God and that you cannot bless sin. So I search my heart today. I lay it open and bare before you. Let your divine searchlight, reveal to my mind and heart, if I have the sin of disobedience in my life. Show me secret sins that are holding back my progress. I want to be blessed!" (Be quiet now and wait on Him to illuminate answers to your mind and heart).

Confess anything he brings to your attention and REPENT of it! Secret sins, unholy affections, closets of selfish things we put **before** God and hold as a type of idol in our life. It can be many things, hey; it's a dirty world out there! Come clean now and you can move forward. I've done this numerous times in my life. It works and I'm a very blessed and highly favored person because of it. You can be too. Trust me on this.

(Write to me and tell me your stories! I'd love to hear them and pray for you!)

Chapter Eight~

CROSSING THE DESERT IN A V.W.

"No one possesses our footprint."

*I*t was a bright sunny day that morning in 1978, as I left Florida headed for Springfield, Missouri. My destination was Central Bible College. There was little money for college in my family's budget but little is much, when God is in it and He always provides when He calls. *My modus operandi?* A 1969 Red Volkswagon Beetle with a distinctive oil leak. I wasn't worried though, I had a case of Pennzoil in the front cargo hold and I was fluent in "dip stick". (wink)

It was a twelve hundred mile trip and it would become another defining moment of my life and a personal sojourn from Egypt, the land of bondage, to Canaan, the land of promise. The trip was an act of obedience and yet another test of my commitment and resolve to follow His voice. I wondered if I'd pass the test.

So, with cardboard boxes stacked to the ceiling and a whopping two hundred dollars in my purse from odd summer jobs, I headed out behind another car of students from my home church who were enrolled at Evangel College, across town from CBC. In the days before cell phones and GPS Navigation systems, we had our route all mapped out using the old school, Rand McNally map. With one overnight stop in Goodlettsville, Tennessee at a family friend's house, we planned to be there by day two.

There was only one problem... I was too embarrassed to tell the other students about the oil-leak in my car, since they were a boy-friend, girl-friend couple and I already felt like a tag-along. Plus, I felt fortunate to have found someone to follow at all, on the two day trip, so I didn't want to be an inconvenience.

Things went smoothly for the first few hours as we headed North and West. But it wasn't long before I lagged behind to put another quart of oil in the motor. I eventually lost sight of them completely (and may I add they didn't seem too concerned) and found myself all alone on this journey from Egypt to Canaan and now left to trust in God. With only my map in hand, I navigated toward Goodlettsville, Tennessee. Looking back, I had a decision to make... I could be pitiful and take on a victim's mentality of "poor little me", or I could "buck up little camper" and start praying like I never had before for God's help!

I chose the latter. "After all, He called me to cross this desert; I could trust Him to get me there to the other side", I reasoned.

By nightfall, weary, hungry and stiff from battling the road all day, I found myself on the outskirts of Goodlettsville. But without my girlfriend Tessa, to guide me, I was lost. I had only the names of a family that we were staying overnight with, but no address. Google didn't exist then, just the phone book… if you could find one or… you could call information from a pay phone, if you had enough change. (Neat)

So, I drove to a 7-Eleven, found a pay phone and called my mother, just like most twenty year old girls would do! Feeling a little sorry for myself, I just needed to hear her voice. "I'm lost, Mom", I lamented. We prayed together. Looking back on it all, I'm sure it was harder on her than me, now that I'm a mother.

I looked up the name of the family in the phone book… No Luck. They weren't listed. "Wow…I'm in trouble", I thought. Then an idea came to me, to go inside the store and ask the cashier if he knew the family name. "Oh that's silly! That would be a one in a million chance." I argued with myself. However, I was out of options, so in I went. "Excuse me, Sir", I said, mustering up all my confidence. "I am scheduled to have dinner tonight with a family from this area and seem to have lost their address. Would you happen to know a family by the name of **Sammy & Peggy Meadows**?" My heart stopped.

"Why Sure!" he chirped, (in that Nashville accent), "Known 'em for years". Gasping, I asked for the directions.

It turned out, that the 7-Eleven was in their neighborhood and I was less than five minutes from their door! (But God)

My eyes were still brimming with tears as my trembling fingers pressed the doorbell of the Meadow's home. A sweet, southern lady answered, her apron sprinkled with flour all over it. The smell of dinner wafted out into the night air along with the sounds of laughter inside. "Come on in, Susie!" She gushed. "We've been expecting you, darl'in"!

That night, I had fried manna for dinner and it never tasted so good!

It never occurred to me to gripe or complain. I was just so **thankful.** God had provided everything I needed. What good would griping and complaining have done me? I never get that, when I read the story of the Israelites.

The next day, before getting on the road, we hugged and kissed and bade our sweet hosts farewell–I would never again see the Meadows family but I'm paying tribute to them here, in my forever-way, for showing the love of Christ to me.

It didn't take long for Tessa and her boyfriend to out run my little sputtering V.W. and they never looked back. It was somewhere in the hills of Arkansas, that I pulled over to a rest stop to put another quart of oil in the engine. I looked up at the blue sky that day and even though I was all alone, in a natural sense, I remember feeling Jesus so very close to me. I was aware of His presence; leading me…all I had to do was **Obey**. As a mother now, I think of all the things that could have happened to a twenty year old woman traveling alone but nothing did. I know **He** was with me. I never saw Tessa again.

By nightfall, I arrived on the grounds of CBC in Springfield, Missouri. I was exhausted beyond belief. It wasn't the four hundred and fifty mile trip that made me so tired. It was from fighting the *Fear of the Unknown.* I pulled in front of the first building I came to, it was Flower Hall. I went inside. An elegant brunette lady sat at the front office desk. "Hello", I said. "I'm Susie McGrath and I've driven all the way from Jacksonville, Florida and I'm here to check into my room please". (My knees were having a fellowship meeting.) She lowered her glasses to the end of her nose and smiled a great, big beautiful smile and said, *"Welcome Home, Susie!"*

And I was…Central Bible College would be my home for the next four years as I trained for the ministry of our Lord Jesus Christ and **Mrs. Dixie (Cox) Sachs**, was the door greeter for Canaan Land that day and didn't even know it.

~~~BRIDE MENTALITY~~~
PART THREE

P.

O.

I. Is For INTEGRITY

S.

E.

D.

Chapter Nine~

NO SHIRT. NO SHOES. NO SERVICE.

"Open the gates to all who are righteous;

and allow the faithful to enter."

Isaiah 26:2 (NLV)

THE PARABLE OF THE MARRIAGE FEAST AND GARMET Matthew 22:2-14 (NLV)

"*T*he Kingdom of heaven can be illustrated by the story of a King who prepared a great wedding feast for his son. When the banquet was ready, he sent his servants to notify those who were invited. But they all refused to come! So, he sent other servants to tell them the feast had been prepared. 'The bulls and fattened cattle have been killed and everything is ready. Come to the banquet.' But the guests he had invited had ignored them and gone their own way, one to his farm another to his business.

Others seized his messengers and insulted them and killed them. The king was furious and he sent out his army to destroy the murderers and burn their town. And he said to his servants, 'the wedding feast is ready, and the guests I have invited aren't worthy of the honor. Now go out to the street corners and invite everyone you see.'

So the servants brought in everyone they could find, good and bad alike and the banquet hall was filled with guests. But when the king came into meet the guests, he noticed a man who **wasn't wearing the proper clothes for a wedding**. (Emphasis added), 'Friend, he asked, how is it that you are here without wedding clothes?' But the man had no reply. Then the king said to the aides, 'Bind his hands and feet and throw him into the outer darkness, where there will be weeping and gnashing of teeth.' For many are called, but few are chosen." **(Words spoken by Jesus)**

It is said that in Eastern cultures, it is the custom to give a preliminary invitation to a feast...much like our "Save the Date", cards today. Then, a more formal invitation would follow announcing the Date, Place and Time. Jesus himself is telling this story in Matthew the twenty second chapter. That's one of the reasons it carries such significance. As we examine it, we can see that first of all, this is a Nuptial Festival set by a Royal father for his son. The father is described as "a certain king" and we can have little doubt that Jesus was referring to His own father, God.

Martin Luther has said of this passage, "The King who made the marriage feast is our heavenly Father; the bridegroom is His son, our Lord Jesus Christ; the bride is the Christian Church, we and all the world, so far as it believes," [20]

Earlier, John the Baptist had referred to Jesus as a "Bridegroom". In fact, John was a type of "Best Man". Listen to his words in **John 3:27-30, (NLV)**

"No one can receive anything unless God gives it from heaven. You yourselves know how plainly I told you, 'I am not the Messiah. I am only here to prepare the way for him.' It is the bridegroom who marries the bride, and the best man is simply glad to stand with him and hear his vows. Therefore, I am filled with joy at his success. He must become greater and greater, and I must become less and less."

Additionally, throughout the Old Testament the union between God and Israel is spoken of under the figure of the marriage covenant and in this parable, there is a hint of something the Apostle Paul broadly stated when he speaks of the Church as the "Wife" of Christ and by John, when he calls her "the Bride, the Lamb's Wife". [21]

Now let's look at the description of the feast itself and get a clearer picture. It was an excellent feast, full of "fat things", abundant quality and quantity. In other words, it was an elaborate spread. We have a fitting description here of the benefits of serving the Lord of Glory! The glorious feast God provides us all with includes:

- Pardon for sin
- Favor with God
- Peace

- Exceeding great and precious promises
- Access to the Throne of Grace
- Comfort of the Holy Spirit
- Assurance of Eternal Life

What a FEAST! To all who would come, whosoever will, **let them come**!

But the tragedy begins to unfold in verse five and we can draw similar parallels to our own modern-day world:

1) The first invitation was returned…"They would not come."

2) The second invitation was more explicit and urgent (vs.4-7). However, their former indifference had now become scorn. They made light of it, going their ways…too busy with their own schedules and life activities. ("Can you hear me now?")

Some of these carried their indifference to the point of aggravated assault! What a strange response to such a generous invitation. The way they have acted was a direct sin against the good king, himself.

Now let me offer further explanation to help you understand something important here. The first two invitations typify the two-fold attempt by Jesus to win Israel. You see, *Jesus came to the chosen people of God, the Jews, first,* but they continually rejected Him as the Messiah. They even went to the length of crucifying Him on the cross. When He died, all things were accomplished for another invitation to go forth, to the Gentiles (through the Apostolic Age).

His servants experienced great cruelty. Many of the Apostles were martyred for their faith. We've seen their tombs and the prisons that held them in Rome, as I alluded to in Chapter Six.

Now what was the reaction of the snubbed king? He was furious and sent his armies against those who had refused his invitations and murdered his servants. The prophetic aspect of this parable was fulfilled in the destruction of Jerusalem, in 70 A.D., when the armies of Titus (Roman Empire) ransacked and burned up the city. (Matthew 23:34; Luke 21:20-24). This parable turns to one of judgment. God used the Roman army as *"the Rod of God's Anger"*, scattering the people who were spared, over the face of the earth. We know this as the <u>Jewish Diaspora</u>.

Bottom line…You don't want to offend God. (Right?)

Now let's look at the third and final invitation:

3) It reveals divine mercy. The king would not be detoured by the ungrateful invitees. He wouldn't call the feast for his beloved son, "OFF". What did he do? He told his servants to go invite anyone, good or bad. Anyone! Invite them to come to the great feast... that's GRACE at work for us, Friends.

So, the invitation went out to the Gentiles, (YEA! That's me). These people were deemed "unworthy" of any privileges by Israel, however, God was now saying, "Let them come in!" [21]

Once in the Kingdom, moral conduct and personal integrity are essential but before entrance, no matter **who** we are, or **what** we've done, we are sinners and need a Savior. In His sight, "there is none good, no not one". All of us have sinned and there is only one way to be saved. Human goodness, mental gymnastics or genetic breeding cannot "EARN" salvation or God's favor and the worst, like the best, are only welcome through the blood of Christ. The Great King has extended His invitation: **"Let Whosoever Will, Come"**!

However, now we come to the necessity of all attendees...the good and the bad, made guests, to *wear the wedding garments.* (Matthew 22:11-14). As the guests arrived, they didn't enter the great hall immediately. Opportunity was given for them to put on appropriate wedding garments provided by the king. (Again, how generous!) It was logical that those gathered from the highways and the byways would be poor and poorly dressed, just like "street people", we see today. So, it was customary in those days in the Eastern parts of the world, to supply royal guests with some simple robe, so everyone present would look uniform. *It was a courtesy but also ensured a certain level of **Integrity**.* [22]

Dear Reader, the wedding garment is a symbol of our personal Integrity before God! *If we don't possess a true desire to live for our Lord that is backed up by a life of dedicated abstinence from the filthiness of sin and the world* (picture Bridezilla), then we don't have the proper garments on **to get in and stay in!** Scripture is clear here. There is no gray area in this. Many modern-day pulpits are twisting or omitting this truth but these words were spoken by Jesus himself, pertaining to who **will** and **will not** be allowed in, to the marriage supper.

Look at the undressed guest in (vs. 11). The king came in and noticed a man who wasn't wearing the proper clothes for a wedding. "Friend", he asked, "How is it that you are here without wedding clothes?" (Remember they had been offered and provided with the invitation), But the man made no reply. He was speechless, without so much as an apology. Why?

> *"Because he did it intentionally. He seems to say, "I am, who I am and No One is going to tell **me** what to do."* (Are you kidding me?)

The wedding garment then, was something conspicuous and distinctive. This was why the king quickly spotted the unrobed man. The garment was not a part of the man's ordinary clothing, but rather a significant sign of loyalty and submission. **To come to the feast without it, was a decisive mark of disloyalty.** He was really no different than those who had refused the king's original invitation was he? Realizing his sin in refusing the king's order, he was speechless and silent as his judgment was pronounced.

> *"Insincerity is robbed of all disguise, when the King enters."* 23

The judgment is pronounced, "Throw him outside, where there will be weeping and gnashing of teeth." Although we live in the **Age of Grace**, (who-so-ever will, may come), we are still required to lay aside our old garments of sin and self-righteousness and clothe ourselves with:

- Repentance
- Humility
- Divine Righteousness through Personal Integrity

The wedding garment is a "Habit of Holiness", so-to-speak. (Picture a catholic nun), only it's as much about how clean our lives are in life-style, as it is about outer appearances. It's not necessarily about a person's hair, make-up, jewelry, etc. as many legalists of old demanded. However, it **is** about modesty. No, those were man's rules imposed on the church and unfortunately an entire generation of people, were negatively affected because there was a **lack of balance.**

True holiness is about the heart first and then about our outward conduct. Paul said in Galatians 5:13, not to use our freedom to satisfy our sinful nature. (vs. 19) of Galatians 5 lists the sins of our sinful (human) nature:

- Sexual Immorality
- Impurity
- Lustful pleasures
- Idolatry
- Sorcery
- Hostility and Quarreling

- Jealousy and Envy
- Outburst of Anger
- Selfish ambition
- Dissention and Division
- Drunkenness and Wild parties

The Apostle Paul goes on to say, "And other sins like these. Let me tell you again, as I have before, that anyone living that sort of life (life-style) will **not** inherit the Kingdom of God". *(Gate Crashers will not be allowed!)*

If men die without such a "wedding garment" they can never participate in the "Marriage Supper of the Lamb", which is only for "Saved Sinners" (aka: Saints). What a terrible sentence has been pronounced here:

"No Shirt–No Shoes–No Service!"

Finally, (vs. 14) Jesus said, "Many are called, but few are chosen" Or…"few choose" as the old preacher, Dwight L. Moody once said. Those who are called but fail to accept Christ will die in their sin. But those who are called and receive Christ, become His "choice ones", and guests in the kings festive house.

Pulpits of America, I exhort you to Preach the Whole Counsel of God's Word to your congregations. We have a sobering responsibility to do so. If we do not, we will be judged more severely because we made little ones, stumble. Jesus told his disciples (His hand-picked Church Leaders), that it would be better for them to have a huge millstone tied around their neck and cast into the sea, than to make one of the Little ones, (unsaved , young converts), stumble.

Our churches are FULL of people who want:

- ***Regeneration without Repentance***
- ***Sanctification without Surrender***
- ***Service without Salvation***

This is the Sin of Presumption! Every sinner must comply with the King's request to put on the proper wedding garment. No exceptions.

*My Study Guide offers prayers that you can pray and space for journaling your private thoughts in this area. I recommend it for church groups or individuals who would like to "come up higher".

Chapter Ten ~

GOT SECRETS?

**"There is nothing hidden that will
not be revealed." Jesus**

Several years ago, September of 2004 to be exact, we had a Church on our annual itinerary commit a generous monthly pledge of five hundred dollars per month to our Ministry and they designated it as a Missions Offering. When the new monthly donation first came in, my husband and I looked at each other and said, "This money is not for us to keep". So, we prayed and asked God to show us where to put it. We were excited to see what He would do. Usually we find out about needs in our lives and then pray that God would provide. However, the scenario was reversed this time and He placed provision in our hands first and we were to find out where to "plug it in". **I call that a "TEST".**

Six months later, we travelled to a new Country we had never been to before. We were invited to come and hold a Spiritual-Emphasis Week for Vienna Christian Center, in Vienna, Austria. We had not met the leadership team there but were referred to them through mutual Career Missionary friends. As we arrived there that cold and snowy March, in 2005, with another couple from the states, Pastors Paul and Kim Owens, from Fresh Start Church, in Peoria, Arizona, we had no idea what we were about to experience.

On Sunday morning we pulled back the curtains in our hotel room and were disheartened to see huge snowflakes coming down in full force. "Oh No, this is going to hinder the crowd today!" I exclaimed to my husband. We are accustomed to that here in the United States. A little weather always affects church attendance here. However, when we arrived at the Church that morning, we were immediately struck by the amount of people in the building. It was **packed out**! We learned that many of the parishioners didn't even own their own vehicle and would come via the metro trains! Wow, that's true dedication! Frankly, their excitement was refreshing.

This church was International in culture, not just for Austrians, per se. At that time, they provided seven services on any given week-end, to accommodate their growing multi-ethnic congregations. It was a little like how I imagined Heaven to be.

Consequently, to accommodate the language barriers, they had installed wireless head-sets in the sanctuary seats and there were translation booths channeled to those head-sets. In this way, everyone could "dial up" their language channel and hear the Gospel of Jesus Christ. It was so cool!

Our ministry was well received and as we visited with our American Missionaries there at the time, we immediately felt the vision of that leadership staff and saw a

GREAT potential harvest to reach multiplied thousands of people throughout Europe from this epicenter of the Gospel. We noticed however, that the missionaries seemed weighed down and pre-occupied.

Now, I'm a bit of a snoop when I sense there's a need out there. I love to connect blessing sources...it's a hobby of mine. So, I pried a little over lunch. However, just meeting us for the first time, they remained pleasant but professional and didn't divulge any personal information. We went back to the hotel to rest before the evening service and felt a heavy burden for them. Not being able to quite put our finger on it, we just prayed for God to lead us and use us in any way He wanted to, that week.

That evening, the service exploded with excitement. It was such a beautiful sight and sound to hear so many ethnicities raising their voices in one-accord, to praise our King of Kings! Again, we were struck by the great potential of this church to reach the nations. After the Sunday evening service, we visited further with these long-term, highly trained and well seasoned missionaries. We pried a little further, asking a few strategic questions. After a little back and forth, we *finally* found out that these missionaries were behind in their monthly budget, by one thousand dollars a month, due to the decline of the money market. Ouch! They had left the U.S. with their funds adequately raised but because the dollar had fluctuated so much on the international market, they were now way off track. Sadly, they were being forced to come back home and itinerate until they could make up the deficit.

Missionaries are unable to work outside jobs in foreign countries due to government restraints, so they are required to raise their yearly budget in advance before ever leaving the U.S. Once these budgets are set, they must remain in place until their next furlough. Simply put, there was no way, outside of a miracle; this couple could make up that kind of deficit on their own. They would have to leave the momentum of what God was doing in the Church there, for six months to a year (however long it took them to raise the funds needed) and risk **missing** a window of opportunity the Church had at its disposal, to go to new spiritual heights and realize some of that potential. This was their dilemma and now God had placed us there with something in our hand... an offering. An offering that had been placed there, six months earlier by a little church in the United States that wanted to make a difference on the Mission Field! It was a no-brainer.

We immediately consulted with our pastor friends that accompanied us from Arizona. They felt led of God to match the five-hundred dollars a month that we had to give, and together we were able to tell those missionaries that the need was met! *Done! Stay at the helm. Don't go back home. See through to completion, what God wants to accomplish through your leadership here!* But the story doesn't end there.

Because this missionary couple was able to remain at their post, Revival continued in that church. It grew so much that they outgrew their facilities. Within the next three years a Building Campaign got under-way. God provided supernaturally. They were able to relocate the main campus to one of the most desirable locations in the entire city and build a great big, beautiful new church, complete with an indoor children's playground! It was like nothing else, **anywhere**, in that city of two million Souls. Hundreds of new converts came to Jesus. Miracles of physical, financial and relational natures were commonplace. God was moving!

We returned each year for a Spiritual- Emphasis week. I distinctly remember one year, after our ministry week concluded, the church continued meeting night after night for an additional thirteen weeks! Hundreds of people were touched by the Gospel of Jesus Christ and what I loved about that was that it was not about any **one man or ministry** but was a corporate outbreak of Spiritual Awakening that was a work of the Spirit and which produced a great harvest. We were so privileged to be a small part of it and it has affected us for eternity. But let me pose a few questions now:

- What if we had kept the money for ourselves? We could have, you know.
- What if we had just told the missionaries; "we are sure sorry about your deficit…we'll be praying for ya."
- Would God have held us accountable for the momentum that was lost and ultimately the Souls that weren't reached because the missionaries had to leave and come back home to raise their funds?
- Would He have met their need through some other means or were **WE HIS INTENDED INSTRUMENT?**
- How many times has the plan of God been thwarted in our lives by a lack of personal Integrity and Greed?

Good food for thought here, isn't it? I'm not sure I can confidently answer all of the above questions accurately but I do know this. More than likely the missionaries would have **had** to come back home to re-raise their budget. That would have affected the Revival and the momentum of the Capitol Campaign. Other provisional miracles might not have taken place because the order of things that happened in that chain of events would have been disrupted and we all know Timing Is Everything.

The truth is, Dear Readers, we **are** His body on this earth. We **are** His Hands extended, reaching out to those in need. We **are** His feet carrying the Gospel message. He places resources in our hands to use **us**! We're not supposed to keep it all for ourselves but basic human nature is greedy and self-serving and it **has been,** from the beginning.

Ultimately, we believe God would have held us accountable at some point in our ministry because of the lack of financial Integrity on our part.

Wise King Solomon said, "Here is the conclusion of the matter; Fear God and Keep His commandments. For this is the duty of all mankind. For God will bring every deed into judgment, including every hidden thing, whether it is good or evil." [24]

Bride Mentality wants to hear, two All Important words from our Lord Jesus when we stand before Him and give an account of what we did on this earth, with what we have been given…"**Well Done"**! That's what the true Bride wants to hear. This should be a huge motivator for us all.

Chapter Eleven~

SHE'S LIKE A DIAMOND

**"A Good Woman is hard to find and
worth far more than Diamonds."
(Proverbs 31:10)**

*F*or two years, I've done an exhaustive study on everything having to do with heavenly and earthly nuptials. I've been intrigued by the entire subject matter, really. Arrested by the Holy Spirit and driven by an insatiable desire to find as many of the hidden parallels that I could, on the subject and connect them here, in this book. One of the things that I've drawn definite spiritual and natural parallels on, are the subject of **Diamonds.**

I love the stone! It's actually a mineral. Remember in my FORWARD that I talked about Genetic Code and said that if it were possible to write out the strands of genetic code for the Church-Bride, we might say that she possessed the DNA of being P.O.I.S.E.D.? Well among those strands, we could also find our Church-Bride has all the qualities of a Diamond. Let's look at them.

The Diamond has many unequaled qualities and is very unique among minerals. Found deep within the earth, it is the hardest known substance in the world. The luster of Diamond is excellent. Diamonds also exhibit great "fire" and brilliance which gives it a shiny, fresh polished look. Due to these factors, the diamond is the most famous of all gemstones on the earth and one of the most expensive. Since it is the hardest substance in the world, it takes a diamond to cut a diamond, thus the use of diamond saw.

The immense hardness of a diamond contributes to its suitability and importance as a gemstone. Because of its hardness, a diamond is immune to scratching and this resistance lends it the ability to withstand daily wear and tear beyond other gemstones. Many gemstones resemble Diamond, however few have its luster, fire and brilliance **and all are softer.** In other words, "Often imitated but never duplicated", as they say.

Now let me draw the spiritual applications because there are some!

The true Church-Bride will withstand the trials and temptations of the End Times. She has a core-value system that makes her rock-solid and handily resistant to daily wear and tear, much like a Diamond. In other words, she can go the distance. She possesses a FIRE of DESIRE for her Bridegroom that makes her stand out, in the big corral of humanity. Her Integrity shines through her because it comes from deep within her, below the surface. It comes from the Glory of the Lord.

However, a diamond is only secure, when it is held in the appropriate prongs of the setting it's mounted in. The prongs must be strong and made of the highest integrity to hold it fast.

Dear Reader, we can possess all the talent, beauty, wealth and fame in the world but the integrity of our personal lives are what lend credibility to them. Personal integrity, which includes holiness, honesty, humility, loyalty, and generosity are the prongs of our life, holding the other gifts and qualities in place.

Many times God uses a gifted and functional person as a vessel He can flow through. He has given them an "assignment". However, if they make poor choices and lose their personal reputation and integrity in the eyes of the collective body of Christ, then their influence will be diminished. This happens even in secular society. God doesn't continue to use those people the **same** way. There are always consequences to sin and we discussed this in PART TWO- OBEDIENCE. Even if that person remains in the Church, they will likely never regain **entirely**, their previous momentum of impact, despite repenting and being forgiven. It's about the law of sowing and reaping.

There are many examples throughout scripture of this. Here are just two of them:

- **David and Bathsheba**–God required his firstborn son. (2 Samuel 12:15-23).

- **Moses breaking the 10 Commandment Tablets** —he was forbidden to go in, to the promise land. (Exodus 32:15-19; Deuteronomy 34:4).

Yes, Personal Integrity is HUGE. Bride Mentality knows this and is vigilant to guard it.

"A good woman is hard to find and worth far more than diamonds." Proverbs 31:10 (NLV)

"A good man obtains favor from the Lord, but a man of wicked intentions He will condemn." Proverbs 12:2 (NLV)

She will be the desire and completion of her bride-groom. He yearns for her. Intercedes for her, laid down His life for her and will come again for her. **What a Great Romance! Jesus and His Church Bride!**

~~~BRIDE MENTALITY~~~
PART FOUR

P.

O.

I.

S. Is For Studied

E.

D.

Chapter Twelve~

LOVE LETTERS

"Study after study has shown that it takes ten years
or ten thousand hours to be great at anything. Ten
thousand hours is the magic number to greatness-
~talent is highly overrated...what really separates
world-class performance from mediocrity is
consistent practice and study!"
Mark Batterson

*A*s a Bible College graduate, my studies necessitated semester-long courses in Old and New Testament Survey, The Synoptic Gospels, The Book of Acts, The Pauline-Epistles, Letters of the Apostles, Peter James and John, The Revelation of Jesus Christ and many others. I completed and passed all these courses of study by God's grace, (not always with flying colors), pulling many "an all-nighter", for those final term-papers. I might add we didn't have computers, powerful software like MS Word and smart devices to search the Web either. We did it "old-school", with type-writers, white-out, correction tape and going to the library to pull dusty, books down off the shelf! (But enough of my sniveling.)

I did it all for one reason, to receive a good grade from my Professor. That was my motivation then.

Not so now. Throughout our ministry and especially these last two years, in preparation for writing this book; I have gotten out many of my old text books (I kept them), blown the dust off, located those Term-papers and rolled up my sleeves out of sheer delight in God's Holy Love Letters. And I have a confession to make here; *I am addicted to God's Word.* There's Divine Revelation in it! You can read the **same** passage several times and get something new out of it each time because of the

"God-Whispers." (Super-LIKE on the God-Whispers!) As the old adage goes, "try it, you'll like it."

Yes, now I study for a far more eternal "grade". I study because I'm in Love with Him. I study to obtain His approval. I study to show Him that HE'S important and valued in my life. I'm speaking of my Bridegroom, Jesus. I have this HUGE CRUSH on Him and I "Get it" that the bible, all sixty-six books of it, are His Love Letters to me... To All of us. I particularly enjoy the New Living Version for everyday pleasure reading but for deeper study, clarity and insight, I refer to many other versions as well.

But I've heard some people say, **"I Hate To Read"**. Well that's fine but if you're truly in love with someone, you'll make an exception to that statement above and read "their" love letters. It's not about reading, it's about loving.

"Study this book of Instruction continually. Meditate on it day and night so you will be sure to obey everything written in it. Only then will you prosper and succeed in all you do." [25]

The bible is the greatest book every written and is **still the #1 Best-Seller!** Oh to have a Best-Seller! It was written over a span of fifteen hundred years by more than forty writers. God moved- on and inspired every single word. He used royalty, shepherds, musicians, prophets and fishermen. The Spirit, who inspired the writers of scripture thousands of years ago, is the **same Spirit** who illuminates readers today. It's written in three different languages, on three different continents and there is no other book like it. And His illumination of scripture is based on His intimate and infinite knowledge of your personality, your circumstances, your dreams, doubts, your history and your destiny. That's why the scripture speaks to us in such kaleidoscopic ways. [26]

Long before there was an "Occupy Wall Street" movement, Martin Luther staged one of the most important protests in history. He upset the Catholic Church and their officials by taking issue with their teaching; that if you paid enough money to the church, you could escape Purgatory (or Hell). So, on October 31, 1517, Luther nailed a long list of complaints called **95 Thesis**, to the front door of the Catholic Church in Wittenburg, Germany. (I've been there and that church still exists today!). These 95 Thesis, spread like wild-fire and helped millions break free from spiritual heresy and know the truth of God's Word about Grace and forgiveness of sin through repentance, for themselves. Luther dared to ask questions people had never dared to ask before. Through him, the Holy Spirit sparked the **Protestant Reformation**. [27] All because someone got in there and dug around the scriptures and studied the bible for themselves!

Here's the realization, it's no different today. If people in our churches were reading and studying God's Word, they would realize the **nonsense** that is being preached in **some** pulpits, today and avail themselves of the EXIT! God's Word of truth is the only match to the prevailing humanistic, logic-system in today's society. To reach the zenith of our potential, we must have a core-value system that comes **only** from being anchored in God's Love Letters.

"Study and be eager and do your utmost to present yourself to God, approved (tested by trial), a work-man who has no cause to be ashamed, correctly analyzing and accurately dividing (rightly handling and skillfully teaching), the Word of Truth." (Amplified Bible) [28]

"I have hidden your word in my heart that I might not sin against you."[29]

Chapter Thirteen~

HELL NO! HEAVEN YES

"Study and Meditate~ That's how we metabolize
God's Word. He wants to write His Story
through your life…
BECOME A TRANSALATION!"

*T*here are a lot of beautiful places in this world. Famous places and others…that are off the radar. Hidden gems waiting to be discovered and explored by us. *But Heaven…now that's a "whole Nutha Level!"* to quote a familiar phrase. The biblical implications about heaven are that it is SO rich in beauty, SO serene, lush, fertile, grandiose, palatial, decadent, over-the-top Ga-Ga-ORGEOUS, that we will run out of adjectives trying to describe how good it is! Our imagination simply cannot do it justice.

Its twelve gates are each made out of a single pearl… Wow! Now that's a whopper of a pearl! I've dedicated Chapter fifteen to the entire subject of "PEARLS". How my heart longs to see it all! *I LOVE secret surprises!*

"The twelve gates were made of pearls–each gate from a single pearl! And the main street was pure gold, as clear as glass." [30]

This is what the scripture is talking about when it says,

"No eye has seen, no ear has heard and no mind has imagined what God has prepared for those who love Him." But it was us that God revealed these

*things to by His Spirit, for His Spirit searches out
everything and shows us God's deep secrets."* [31]

Here's the Reality, unfortunately there will always be
people who deny the existence of Heaven and Hell. The
thought of an after-life agitates them to the point that they
find comfort in denial. Why?

I believe it's because they aren't ready for Eternity.

What we're not prepared for, or don't understand, we
tend to have an aversion to. Human nature fears and
dreads the unknown. When a person doesn't know Christ,
they tend to have a general hostility or detestation towards
heaven. It makes them uncomfortable. Perhaps you have
heard people joke or even brag about how they can't wait
to go to Hell so they can join the ultimate party. Really?
**"Does weeping and gnashing of teeth (violent anger),
sound like a fantasy of frolicking fun to you?"**
Ummmmmmm, that would be a NO.
Seriously, when you know the King of Glory, your Soul
desires to see Him! Heaven becomes a desired destination. Hell, the place to avoid. Satan is lying to lost people.
That's what he does. He's done the same old things for

centuries. (Geez, you'd think he would throw in something new once in a while). But he uses the same old tricks because *THEY WORK*. (Hello?)

I don't mean to underplay him here. His tactics have become effective against humanity, for centuries, so he continues to use them.

I develop this subject of *Taking Dominion over our enemy*, in PART SIX but to my point, people who don't know Jesus as Savior and Lord of their lives are actually being lured toward Hell by demonic forces, much like my Dad. Hell is a place of eternal damnation and torment. Eternal Separation from God. There is never any going back or coming out. It's forever and there's no "Open-bar, party" being provided. *"It's a Dry County!"*

Modern-day pulpits rarely discuss Hell or judgment, or even repentance from Sin, for that matter...It's not making the Gospel "palatable", they reason. We're too worried we might offend somebody. However, this grieves the Spirit of God because when we as church leaders keep **consequence before the people,** it enlightens them. This in turn, motivates people to "police their own lives". It's human nature to want to transgress the law. All you have to do is get out on an open highway, in a new car, to see how human nature exerts itself. However, **when we know how**

far is "too far", and what the consequences are, the majority of folks will come under submission to Authority.

Dear Reader, if you're reading this and our discussion about people denying heaven and bragging about Hell describes you; will you please go find a private spot (right now), where you can pray and ask Jesus to come into your heart? Ask him to forgive you for all your mistakes, sins, foolish behavior, even rebellion to Him. (You name it) And to wash you clean with His precious blood. Blood that was spilled out for you, when He took your place and died on that cross. I assure you, He will!

Good News! He Loves you! He Loves You so much! Now after you've prayed that prayer, get a Bible or Bible App (that you can download to your smart phone) and *START READING GOD'S LOVE LETTERS!* You've got some catching up to do. I recommend beginning your reading in the Book of John first because it's easy to understand for new Christians. Start studying God's Word! Get a daily devo, bible study (like mine…shameless plug), and *GET GROWING!*

And please, if you prayed that prayer, write to me @ the address in the back of this book and I promise, I'll pray over you and will do my very best to respond. I love you, Dear Reader.

~~BRIDE MENTALITY~~~
PART FIVE

P.

O.

I.

S.

E. Is For Eyes Focused

D.

Chapter Fourteen~

THE BELIEVER'S EYE

**"It's more than what you're looking at…
it's also about PERSPECTIVE.
You can look without ever seeing."**

I recently read an article on the importance of "Batter's Eye." It relates the story of a little league team and their parents' visit to the Texas Ranger Ballpark, in Arlington, Texas.

As they walked out onto the field, the tour guide asked the team if they knew where the Batter's Eye was located. Then with the skill of an old story teller, he leaned in to the circle he had assembled around home plate and revealed to the group the location and purpose, of the batter's eye. He explained that if you looked past the pitcher's mound and above the center field fence, you will see a large area of green grass. "That's the batter's eye", he said in a whisper "and every big league ball park has one and they are always located in the same spot. They are extremely important, and the batters are thankful for them", he continued with some steel in his voice. "It is to give the batter a clear and undistracted view of the ball as it leaves the pitcher's hand. It is to protect the batter from being hit by a ball he is not able to see or cannot locate." the tour guide explained.

This is reminiscent of how the Psalmist used the analogy in Psalm 119:105, to explain how the Lord provides a clear and undistracted view of the path He has chosen for each of us. Here in this verse, scripture states that the Word of the Lord (His Love Letter, to us), is a lamp to our feet and a light to our path. Suffice to say, this lamp will never go out for lack of oil, for it is divinely lit by the inspiration and anointing of God.

Major league batters may use a blank background to gain clarity as to which pitch they will swing at–the split finger, fast ball or slow curve. However, as Spirit-led believers, we have the Word of the Lord to bring a clear and undistracted view of the way we are to walk. In holiness, in harmony during harrowing times of trial and tribulation and as to how we can always keep our confident hope in His imminent return. We can call **this** the "**Believer's Eye!**" [32]

"And since you don't know when that time will come, be on guard! Stay Alert! "The coming of the Lord can be illustrated by the story of a man going on a long trip. When he left home, he gave each of his servant's instructions about the work they were to do, and he told his gatekeeper to watch for his return. You too, must keep watch! For you don't know when the master of the house will return–in the evening, at midnight, before dawn or at daybreak. Don't let him find you sleeping when he arrives without warning. I say to you what I say to everyone: Watch for Him!" [33]

In the above passage from Mark the thirteenth chapter, three different words are used for "watch". The first word has to do with the physical sight as opposed to blindness. Jesus said, "When you see these things coming to pass, look up." We are to use our physical sight to be aware of things going on around us.

The second word refers to being *awake and watchful.* This word is sometimes connected with prayer. Again Jesus told His disciples to watch and pray so they would **not** fall into temptation.

The third word is similar in meaning to the first two with the added idea of not only using our physical sight and being watchful but staying that way. We are to keep our eyes open and stay awake. We are to stay vigilant! When we realize that Jesus gave this command to "watch"; in the context of His second coming, this word takes on an added significance. How about you?

- Are you staying Sober minded and Alert for the coming of the Lord?
- Do you let "this world distract you", from thinking about His return?
- Are your eye's looking up to the Eastern sky, as often as you can, mindful that there will be the sound of the trumpet blast, just before we are

"Raptured or Caught Away", to go with Him to our Marriage Supper?

Don't Forget to Be Watching for Jesus' Return, Everyday! The Apostle Peter reinforces Jesus' comment to "watch" by saying:

"Stay Alert! Watch out for your great enemy, the devil, he prowls around like a roaring lion, looking for someone to devour." [34]

Chapter Fifteen~

THE PEARL OF GREAT PRICE

"Since the death of Christ, the Holy Spirit has been
calling to each new generation of men and women
on earth, adding those who would *answer with obedience*, to the Church which He has been building
for more than twenty centuries. Ah, it takes time
to produce the Pearl of Great Price!"

*P*icture a string of pearls. Do you ever stop to wonder which part of the fathomless depths of water, in this world, your treasure has come from? Some pearls come from salt water, other from fresh but all are searched out from a hidden place deep below the surface. Ahhhh, here is where our story begins!

The Parable of the Pearl (Matthew 13:44-45) NLV

"The Kingdom of Heaven is like a treasure that a man discovered hidden in a field. In his excitement, he hid it again and sold everything he owned to get enough money to buy the field."

"Again, the Kingdom of Heaven is like a merchant on the lookout for choice pearls. When he discovered a pearl of great value, he sold everything he owned and bought it!" (**Words spoken by Jesus**)

In these beautiful passages, the merchant as well as the buyer who finds the pearl and sells all he has to buy it, represents one and the same figure. None other than Christ himself. This merchantman that Jesus portrays, was a connoisseur and knew all about pearls. He had discernment and knowledge as to their real worth and could not be deceived by any sham production. Assessing their value, he paid the price and never regretted his purchase because he knew he was getting "the real deal".

The Kingdom of Heaven and the Church, represent the present Christian dispensation with its partial success and with the continued presence, (until the end of the age), of the wheat, side by side, with the tares[35] (or weeds); Bridezilla, the Luke-warm church, along-side the true Bride of Christ. In other words, we go to church together right now. We aren't separated yet. (Oh Goody)

"Christ loved the Church and gave Himself for it and she will ever be the object of His Desire."

This same church is *one* pearl, *one* body composed of many members; **men and women alike for we know that "Bride of Christ", is a gender-neutral term**. *One* Habitation of God, through the Spirit, though built of many stones; *one* as the purchase of Christ's all-atoning blood; *one* as the workmanship of the eternal spirit whose ministry it is to fashion the Church into one body. [35]

This Church, Jesus said He would build, is composed of all regenerated Jews and Gentiles from Pentecost till the return of Christ, as the Bridegroom for His Bride–the Church of the living God.

Does it not pass all comprehension to realize Christ's *DESIRE* for us? And that even when we were enemies He died to possess us because His desire was toward us. Can we even wrap our mind around that kind of **LOVE**? (I'm trying)

Listen to this **stunning depiction** of the Christ-Bride in Psalms~

"Listen to me, O Royal daughter; take to heart what I say. Forget your people and your family far away. For your Royal husband delights in your beauty; honor Him, for He is your Lord."

"The bride, a princess looks glorious in her golden gown. In her beautiful robes, she is led to the King, accompanied by her bridesmaids. What a joyful procession as they enter the King's palace! Your sons will become Kings, like their father. You will make them rulers over many lands. I will bring honor to your name in every generation. Therefore, the nations will praise you forever and ever."[36]

The very word *Pearl* is derived from a Sanskrit word meaning: *Pure*. So finding the valuable pearl, the merchantman "sold all he had", to possess it. No sacrifice was too great to have this lustrous pearl in the palm of His hand, as His very own.

A fact of interest regarding a real pearl, is that it is a product of a *living organism*, which is not true of any other precious stone, whether sapphires, diamonds, rubies or emeralds. The pearl is produced *as a result of an injury suffered by a living organism, such as an oyster.* The reason a pearl is produced is because of the presence of an outside substance such as a grain of sand, an egg of either the mollusk or an outside parasitic intruder. [37]

As nature would have it, the oyster begins to manufacture a calcareous matter (characteristic of calcium), in thin layers and spreads it over the intruding object until ultimately it assumes a pearly luster. Therefore, in the process of its making, the living organism surrounds the foreign matter with mother-of-pearl, (also called nacre), until gradually the pearl is formed. Out of much suffering an object of beauty is produced. The offending particle becomes the Pearl of Great Worth!

This story is reminiscent of the fact that we the Church-Bride came out of the wounded bruised and battered Body of Christ! This is a great mystery, just like the story of a pearl in an oyster shell. Through His travail and pain, He covered us with His attoning blood "making a thing of beauty". An object of desire and great worth.

The Pearl is developed ever so slowly over a span of time. So it is, with God's Church-Bride. Since the death of Christ the Holy Spirit has been calling to each new generation of men and women on earth, adding those who would answer with obedience, to the Church which He has been building for more than twenty centuries. Ah, it takes time to produce the Pearl of Great Price!

The Holy Spirit is producing the treasure, occupied with her purification, so that she may be presented to the King of Kings and Lord of Lord's as being without spot or wrinkle, washed in the blood of the Lamb. Just like my beautiful picture on the front cover of this book! **(James Nesbit, Artist)**

"Christ loved the Church; He gave up His life for her to make her holy and clean, washed by the cleansing of God's word. He did this to present her to himself as a glorious church without spot or wrinkle or any other blemish. Instead, she will be holy and without fault." [38]

Dear Reader, we will never know all that it cost Jesus to bring the Church into being! None of the ransomed will ever know **all** that was involved in the price He paid to have a redeemed people as "His pearl". Though He was rich…He became poor. He had no money to buy us with, so He gave the only thing of value that He possessed… *His own precious, sinless life.* With His own blood, He bought her. What Love! What Desire! What Romance! Our heavenly merchantman paid for the creation of His glorious church with own death on the cross. (Shout Now!)

No One has ever done for us, what Jesus did. So what does He want in return?

Our Desire~ Our Devotion~ Our Romance~

"And I will make an everlasting covenant with them: I will never stop doing good for them. I will put a DESIRE (emphasis added), in their hearts to worship me, and they will never leave me." [39]

Chapter Sixteen~

PILLOW TALK

**"The More You Love God, the More
He Reveals His Secrets to You.**
It's a Form of Pillow Talk".

I love my guy! And one of our favorite things to do, at the end of a long day is to lay side by side, on each other shoulder and share whatever comes to mind, in those last few moments before drifting off to sleep. Sometimes we share our hopes and dreams for the future, or pray together over some pressing need. Other times, we can get tickled over something and will laugh uncontrollably over the silliest things! In fact, we laugh...**A LOT**! And we tell each other things..."Pillow Talk", they call it. *It's a form of intimacy and marriages should have it.*

Correspondingly, I believe that God wants to share intimacy with his Church-Bride. The more we Love Him, the more we read His Love Letters, (the Bible), Study, Pray and Meditate; the more connected we become in our affections **for** Him; and *the more **He** reveals to us... through God-whispers.* It's a Reward for our devotion. He loves it. It's pleasing to Him and he reveals secrets that affect our quality of life and destiny...*It's HIS form of pillow talk, you might say, and it's beautiful!*

In fact, much of this book constitutes my own pillow talk with my "First-Love", Jesus. What He's whispered to me, to create this book for you, His Church-Bride, is that *He wants supernatural intimacy with His Bride that goes deeper than the level of **any other** human relationship* *we possess.* The fact that the infinite God of the Universe would pay our ransom through the shed blood of His only begotten Son, just to win us back from serving a "justified" sentence of eternity in Hell, is mind boggling to me; but that's Him! That's what He did! *He's Our Great Avenger.* Oh, How I Love Him! And I'm returning His love, by giving Him ALL **my** devotion.

I like to teach it this way:

God has only one need~ to be needed by us.

Yes, our God ***created*** intimacy and He desires for us, His people to draw close to Him and pour out our hearts..."He's all ears." (Let's re-read the scripture below)

"And I will make an everlasting covenant with them: I will never stop doing good for them. I will put a DESIRE (emphasis added), in their hearts to worship me, and they will never leave me." [39]

I challenge you, if you haven't made Him your *Number One.* Your intimate *"First-Love"*, the one you run to first, with *Everything...Then what in **this** world, are you waiting* *for?* Once you do, you'll never go back to causal Religion... Sunday morning only... leave-it-at-the-door, Christianity.

- **Do You Feel Stuck? Then Take my Challenge.**

You'll be amazed at how things start moving in your life! The answers to prayer that will take place and the peace and fulfillment you will enjoy from His Presence will be AHHHHMAZING!

Yes, I'm a blessed woman, who is happily married but I've made the statement to people that "**Jesus is my husband, first.**"

Why would I do that? Isn't that kind of weird?

Not at all. Not when you consider that there is NO WAY my earthly husband could ever meet all my needs, fill all the voids in my life or heal the brokenness of my past. As much as he loves me, he can't do that for me. And vice-versa, I can't do that for him either. Because we're not God! Only God can do some things for us. That's why we need to make Him our "First Love."

In my **FORWARD**, I mentioned the fact that taking this step is going to be difficult for some, more than others because of past baggage they have with respect to relationships. *But God can heal any brokenness!* I'm a perfect example of that. Sometimes our perspective has been skewed because we live in this fallen place. We live in a place where people break their promises and don't keep their vows. Where people change and fall in and out of love. But God is not like that! He keeps His word to us and He NEVER Changes.

As we discussed previously, when we allow ourselves to "Re-think" the word "Marriage", when we let go of our *experience,* (especially if it's been negative), we can defy the status-quo on the whole cycle of marriage. Let me recount that cycle here. The **typical** marriage cycle we've encountered over the last thirty years of full-time itinerant ministry, is as follows: (doesn't include everyone but it's the **vast majority**).

- Couple Meets
- Couple Falls In Love
- Couple Marries
- Kids Come
- Kids Grow Up and Fly the Nest
- Marriage Drifts Apart
- Couple Falls Out of Love
- Divorce or Affairs Occur or…(Just as Bad)

- Couple Stays Together but Lives *Separate Lives* with **No** Intimacy *(which includes **all** forms of communication; not just sexual intimacy)*

We see this **A Lot**…and "Me No Likey!" If I had a dollar for all the couples we've seen like this in our travels, I could retire and probably move to Tahiti. (*I love palm trees*)

So, Here's Some Food For Thought:
- **What if being married to the same lover never lost its attraction?**
- **What if being married to the same lover got even better with the passing of time?**

It can. (Now, I can just hear some of you saying right now, "Uhhhh Right, you're not married to the piece of work I am!") No, I'm not. But I **am** married to someone that isn't perfect and neither am I!

But the secret to Bride-Mentality, is putting Jesus First, as our "First-Love" and in order for marriage to work and **stay working**, we have to have this triangle, with Christ as the Head. *Both partners* need to place Jesus as their Number One. It's the **only way** our earthly marriages will stand the test of time, without running out of intimacy.

Then and only then, can we receive healing in all the other relationships of our lives. Both partners need to come on board with this for earthly, hetero-sexual marriage to succeed the way God intended it to succeed.

So even though this book is not a Marriage and Family book in the natural sense of the words, there **are overlaps** with the Bride-Mentality I'm teaching here. *My purpose isn't to try to "fix every failing marriage out there, through this book* (even though that would be nice). *My purpose* is to make us aware that we may be bringing **biases** into our relationship with God because we've been hurt by human beings.

If any of you, Dear Readers, are inadvertently doing this; correcting this negative behavior will help your relationships with God. You see, "Church-Bride, Mentality", alters our human mind-sets, thinking patterns and belief systems regarding marriage, **to guard against contaminants** that will try to "seep in". And there are many forms of relational contaminants out there; such as past abuse (of many kinds), abandonment, infidelity, or a spouse that manipulates through control, etc.

But our heavenly marriage-partner, Jesus, is not flawed like PEOPLE. He's perfect! (*Can I hear the Angel Choir, Now?)* We can trust that He will not abandon us, abuse us, manipulate us or hurt us in any other way, like humans beings do to one another. This frees us to allow God **"In"**, to private areas of our life regarding love and intimacy. So, whether you are a Single person or a Married person, if **any of us** are "stingy-spirited" with one another, unforgiving, *not* giving, not serving, etc. **that will creep in to, and affect how we love and serve our Lord**! (Cricket, cricket).

And, I'd venture to say that if we have no home-fires burning and **are** "stingy-spirited" with one another, the prayer-closet is cold, too! (Just Say'in)

It's time to rebuild the marriage! *Make that baby into a **triangle** with Christ being the Head. And it's time to re-kindle lost intimacy with our Lord.* Let's get our Eyes **off** of our problems and refocus them **on** Jesus. *Remember Bridezilla, she focused her eyes on everything else but her Bridegroom!* Give Him your undivided attention, devotion and love. He wants to be our strong arm but we have to give Him something to work with...we have to give Him **US!**

"And I will give them singleness of heart and put a
new spirit within them. I will take away their stony,
stubborn heart and give them a tender responsive

heart, so they will obey my decrees and regulations. Then they will truly be my people and I will be their God." (Ezekiel 11:19-20)

Here are examples of how King David did Pillow Talk with his God:

"In the morning, O Lord, you hear my voice. In the morning, I lay my request before you and wait in expectation." (Psalm 5:3 NLV)

"All night long I search for you, in the morning I earnestly seek for God." (Isaiah 26:9 NLV)

Chapter Seventeen~

WANTED! BRIDEZILLA... NOT ARMED! NOT DANGEROUS!

"We will follow after other Lovers no more

but will return to our first-Husband."

Hosea 2:5 (NLV)

The Parable of the Faithless Wife–
(Hosea 2:2&3, 13)

(Vs. 2) "But now bring charges against Israel–your mother, for she is no longer my wife, and I am no longer her husband.

Tell her to remove the prostitute's make-up from her face and the clothing that exposes her breasts.

(Vs. 3) Otherwise, I will strip her naked as the day she was born.

(Vs. 13) I will punish her for all those times when she burned incense to her images of Baal (Idol god), when she put on her earrings and jewels and went out to look for her lovers but forgot all about me", says the Lord.

Wow! This is a little hard to read. We see a jealous God for His people, Israel here. There are various metaphors used in the bible to represent God's association with and care of, His people: but the most sacred and enduring of them all is that of a marriage covenant. Examples of this abound throughout the bible. (Exodus 19:3-6; 20:2-6; 34:14; Isaiah 54:5; Ezekiel 16; 2 Cor. 11:2 & Ephesians 5:21-23).

Jeremiah devoted entire chapters to Israel the adulterous wife, invited to be reconciled to her divine husband.

"You have prostituted yourself with many lovers, so why are you trying to come back to me?" says the Lord.

"Look at the shrines on every hilltop. Is there any place you have not been defiled by your adultery with other gods? You sit like a prostitute beside the road waiting for a customer. You sit alone like a nomad in the desert. You have polluted the land with your prostitution and your wickedness. That's why even the spring rains have failed, for you are a brazen prostitute and completely shameless. Yet you say to me, 'Father, you have been my guide since my youth.' [40]

Hosea likewise, uses this similar analogy with the addition of an adulterous wife, which signified the Jewish nation and her unfaithfulness. Idololatry, sensuality and material excess prevailed. (Sound familiar?) The worship of the true God had been degraded into calf-worship (one made out of molten gold) and then to Baal–worship of the Canaanites. (The land they moved to from Egypt). This form of spiritual idolatry consisted in loving and serving the creature more than the creator. Therefore, covetousness and sensuality are spoken of under that term. (Romans 1:25; Colossians 3:5; & Philippians 3:19).

The prophet Isaiah also speaks out:

"Such stupidity and ignorance! Their eyes are closed, and they cannot see. Their minds are shut, and they cannot think. The person who made the idol never stops to reflect, "Why, it's just a block of wood! I burned half of it for heat and used it to bake my bread and roast my meat. How can the rest of it be a god? Should I bow down and worship a piece of wood?" [41]

Unfortunately, this was not only a picture of backslidden Israel but also of today's modern Luke-warm Church… none other than **Bridezilla**. She has a form of godliness but not power to back it up.

Hello? We cannot have divided affections…that's called Idolatry.

We have to Love HIM, Church! This is in the DNA of the **True Bride of Christ**. She Loves **HIM**. But contrast that with Bridezilla…the Luke-warm church, who is having an **adulterous affair with the world**! Bridezilla has many lovers...riches, fame, quest for power, material possessions, addictions of sex, substances, etc. and a lust to be entertained. *She always needs to be entertained because it's **All about "Her"***. (Oh Em Geeee)

Now, keep that image in the back of your minds as you serve the Lord. It will help you to stay on course. **Remember: Bridezilla will be left behind!**

I think the Apostle, Paul said it best, as he warned young Timothy:

"You should know this Timothy that in the last days there will be very difficult times; for people will love only themselves and their money. They will be boastful and proud, scoffing at God, disobedient to parents and ungrateful. They will consider nothing sacred. They will be unloving and unforgiving; they will slander others and have no self-control. They will be cruel and hate what is good. They will betray their friends, be reckless, be puffed-up with pride and love pleasure rather than God. They will act religious, but they will reject the power that could make them godly. **Stay away from people like that!**" (Emphasis added). [42]

In the final fourteenth chapter of the book of Hosea, God sends a final, loving, tender plea to His beloved,

"O Israel, stay away from idols! I am the one who answers your prayers and cares for you. I am like a tree that is always green; all your fruit comes from me. Let those who are wise, understand these things. Let those with discernment, listen carefully. The paths of the Lord are true and right and righteous people live by walking in them. But in those paths, sinners stumble and fall." (Vs. 8-9)

- **What truly characterizes us as the Bride-Church, God's Chosen People?**
- **How shall we describe what His Bride looks like?**

We will be known by our Focused EYES. She doesn't flirt with the world.

Bride-Church: Is P.O.I.S.E.D.

1) Has Intimacy in **Prayer**
2) **Obeys** His Commands
3) Has a Heart to follow through on the details~**Integrity**
4) Loves Instruction-**Study**
5) Has singleness of **Eyes** &Heart and Desires only Him
6) Walks in **Dominion** over the enemy

- **How can we EXCEL against such a backdrop of expectation?**

Through guarding our hearts and minds from Seducing Spirits.

7 Ways to Seduce-Proof Your Life:

1) Never Stop Being Thankful! (Rejoice in the Lord Always)
2) Rejoice Evermore (See #1)
3) Abstain from the appearance of Evil (No Casinos, No Bars, No mind altering, addictive substances, no nakedness...dress modestly, being careful that we do **nothing** to cause a brother or sister to stumble)
4) Pray without Ceasing
5) Don't Quench the Spirit!
6) Test Everything and Every Person you come in contact with, to see if they are Good or Bad. (you'll know them by their fruits)
7) Never Think **YOU** are above being Seduced!

Our Bride picture reveals a Church that is:

- Revived (brought back to life),
- Wise (she's learned from her mistakes)

- Joyful (she's notified her face)
- Pure (washed in the blood of the lamb)
- Fair (Beautiful!)

She is His Queen and He desires her more than the finest gold and more than the sweetest honey! What a great lavishness of reward awaits the Redeemed of All Ages! His Bride Church...**Here Comes the Bride**!

"And I will give them singleness of heart and put a new spirit within them. I will take away their stony, stubborn heart and give them a tender, responsive heart, so they will obey my decrees and regulations. Then, they will truly be my people and I will be their God". [43]

~~~BRIDE MENTALITY~~~
PART SIX

P.

O.

I.

S.

E.

D. Is For Taking Dominion

Chapter Eighteen~

THE WARRIOR IS A GRANDMA!

"In Touching God's Authority, we touch God Himself. God's work basically is done not by power but by Authority."

Watchman Nee

She was seventy-five years old and her bones creaked a little, as she walked out of the church service that Wednesday night, in Rogers County, Oklahoma. Arthritis, "Arthur" as she called it, had settled in, to almost all her joints making normal navigation more and more difficult. However, "Mama Purkey" (as she was affectionately called), was not easily detoured. Part Cherokee Indian, she was known as one of the most persistent women in those parts. She was still humming the last song they had sung that night in church ("Standing on the Promises"[44]), as she entered her little white frame house, on January 14, 1980.

No sooner has she settled into her favorite robe and slippers but the phone began to ring. Answering the telephone was one of Minnie Cordia Purkey's favorite pastimes. A worried voice sounded on the other end of the phone line. It was her son, Bill. "What's that?" She said. "They think Mark Ray has cancer? Lymphoma, they think? Yes, yes, of course I'll go to prayer." (Click)

Mama wasted no time when an urgent prayer request came to her attention. She was most certainly a prayer warrior and with her Indian heritage, she knew how to go on the "War Path" in prayer!

"Mark Ray", as she called him, was the fifth of six grandsons she was blessed with. Already enrolled as a college freshman at Evangel University in Springfield, Missouri; it seemed nineteen year old Mark had scarcely gotten through high school graduation and all the college offers he'd received for being a highly decorated athlete in three sports and now he had cancer? It seemed impossible. Yes, It seemed impossible that he could have an admitting diagnosis of: *Right Hilar and Right Paratracheal Adenopathy with possible Lymphoma*, looming over his life…but after a week of exhausting tests, he did. What started as a "pesky cough" had now turned into a hospital admission at St. John's Medical Center in Tulsa, Oklahoma and dreadful news.

So, armed with the song, "Standing on the Promises", fresh in her mind, Mama Purkey went to prayer. As she finished brushing her thick, white hair, she looked up at the clock on the wall…it said Eleven o'clock p.m. She began to pray.

She asked for God's divine intervention for her grandson. She just wasn't accepting this negative report but was appealing to a higher power…the Great Physician, Jesus himself. Then, she began rebuking sickness, infirmity and disease from his body, using the mighty name of

Jesus, as a weapon of warfare. Continuing, she quoted a key healing passage:

"Yet it was our weakness he carried; it was our sorrows that weighed Him down. And we thought His troubles were a punishment from God, a punishment for His own sins! But He was pierced for **our** rebellion, crushed for **our** sins. He was beaten so **we** could be whole and whipped so **we** could be healed." [45] (emphasis added)

As she prayed the promises in God's Word, she recounted later that she felt God's Spirit direct her to *"Stand On My Word!"* So, she prayed a little louder..."FATHER, I Come to you in Jesus name, standing on your promises"...but the Spirit interrupted her again and said, *"Stand On My Word!"*

Not discouraged, she increased her volume and intensity again, "FATHER! I COME TO YOU IN THE NAME OF JESUS..." But a third time, a still, small voice gently repeated the earlier command to, ***"Stand on My Word!"***

So, Mama Purkey said she did the only thing left, that she could think of and picked up the large, old, Family Bible that lay resting on her coffee table, and plopped it out in the middle of the living room floor! Opening it up to the passage in Isaiah 53, she carefully got up on top of the bible, STOOD ON IT and began praying! At seventy-five years of age, she wrangled with the powers of Heaven and Hell and prayed like someone decades younger.

Meanwhile, over at St. John's Medical Center, thirty miles away, Mark was having difficulty falling asleep, in his hospital bed. His chest felt like it was on fire and the pain increased with every persistent cough. There was no one in the room now and he felt the Spirit of FEAR creep over him and arrest him with an icy grip. The doctor's words to him just a few hours earlier, rang relentlessly in his ears, "this cancer has spread like wild-fire."

The Fear Grew Bigger.

In fact, it engulfed him, until the star athlete lay trembling in bed. All alone, he felt isolated and helpless. As he lay there, he heard the sound of the large, solid, wood hospital door swing open. He looked up, to greet his parents who, he suspected had arrived but No One was there. The door was still shut. "Perhaps I imagined it", he thought to himself. However, he immediately became aware of a "real" presence in the room. In fact, the presence was moving around his bed. A very real presence, though unseen, was moving up one side of his bed, around the foot-board and back up to his right side!

Then, oddly...intentionally, the presence stopped. It was so real; he thought he might reach out and feel someone. He groped the air but felt nothing tangible. Instinctively he knew it was the Spirit of God, having been raised in a Spirit-filled, Christian Church. He felt the Lord dealing with him regarding a call to ministry he'd accepted as a young boy at Kids Camp, in Turner Falls, Oklahoma but had ignored in the wake of success in sports and all the college offers. He began to weep. Through tears, he repented of his own rebellion to the call of God on his life to preach the Gospel.

Suddenly, Mark felt a very warm hand lay on his chest. It was **extremely** warm and felt good to him, since he had been laying there cold and shaking, just moments earlier. The hand pressed directly over his heart. It was a very large, right hand and he could feel the palm and long fingers...even a thumb. His shaking stopped. Peace! It felt warm and peaceful. It only laid there for a few seconds, then, lifted and as suddenly as it had come, the presence moved toward the door and he heard the sound of it open and close again but No One was there. "Am I dreaming?" Mark said to himself and drifted off to sleep.

Back at the house, thirty miles away, Mama Purkey had lost all track of time. She knew she had been praying a while; however, she was shocked when she finally stopped and looked at the clock again...it said six o'clock a.m. "Surely not!" she thought to herself. But it was and she had prayed all night, standing on God's Promises!

The next morning, she hurried to shower and dress, so she could get to the hospital on time. It was scheduled to be a radical surgery involving the removal of several large, black masses of tumors, revealed on the X-rays that were dangerously encroaching upon Mark's heart, lungs and trachea. The team of specialists included head surgeon, R.W. (Tex) Goen, Jr. He advised the family that morning what the plan would be. They would make a small incision in Mark's throat and do a Mediastinoscopy to obtain a biopsy of the first mass. Pathologists would be standing by, to ascertain an immediate finding of malignancy, if applicable. If no diagnosis was attainable with the frozen section, then a second, radical surgery would have to be undertaken. *A Right Anterior Thoractomy* would ensue, which would require going in on the right side, and breaking Mark's ribs in two, in order to access the large tumors scattered and wrapped throughout the chest cavity. An arduous procedure to say the least, involving a lung specialist as well, the prognosis for full recovery would be grim at best. However, a nineteen year old young man, in peak physical condition prior to this on-set, certainly warranted the maximum effort.

The family and friends huddled in the
waiting room praying.

As Mama Purkey arrived at the hospital that Thursday morning, January 15, 1981, she was still praying under her breath. She was running a little late as she entered the hall corridor, where Mark's room was located. His hospital bed was already out in the hall, to be wheeled into surgery. She called out urgently, "Wait, just a minute!" As she approached his bedside, she said, "I need to see my Grandson." They waited. Standing over him, with tears in her eyes, she asked, *"Did He Touch You?"*

"Yes, Mama!" Mark replied, their hands now clasped tightly. *"I felt a hand lay on my chest,"* he whispered. Patting him, she lowered her voice and said, *"Well good, Mama loves you way too much."* And then, with a satisfied look on her face, and praising God loud enough for anyone to

hear, she turned and headed toward the waiting room to join the others.

Minutes later, Dr. Goen opened Mark's neck to scope the mass for a biopsy. The X-rays hung on the adjacent wall for easy reference and clear evidence of what they were dealing with. As they removed the first right Hilar (lung) mass, measuring 7x5 cm in diameter, and then a second, smaller mass which measured 1 cm and was ill-defined in the right lung, mid-field lateral to the Superior (or top portion), of the right lung, the findings were interpreted as being most consistent with a neoplasm; with consideration being lymphoma. These were immediately removed and a biopsied frozen section was sent to the nearby lab. No further masses were identified and the first incision was closed!

Here were the findings from the pathology report, included in the medical records that we still have in our possession today. Pathological findings revealed a benign tumor with casketing granulomatous inflammation with necrosis consistent with Tuberculosis. However, neither a TB test nor Fungus test came up with conclusive evidence of any identifiable strain both initial and subsequent.

The Bottom line, in layman's terms…they couldn't find anything!

Nothing life-threatening…after all the experts suspected the **worst,** based on three days of exhaustive diagnostic tests and the finest educated diagnosis available at that time. The primary diagnosis was Non-Hodgkin's Lymphoma but when they got inside, there were only two benign tumors…the Work of God's Unseen Hand!

We refer to these medical records from time to time, during times of crisis and trial, to remind us of an Awesome God, A Great Physician, Jesus, who *still answers the effectual fervent prayer of righteous men and women*!

Had it not been for a praying Grandmother, and many, many others who **knew how** to engage in spiritual warfare and take dominion over sickness and disease, this story could have ended quite differently for this nineteen year old young man named, Mark R. Purkey.

I'm happy to report that "Mark Ray" not only answered that call of God, to preach the gospel, by enrolling that Spring, 1981, at Central Bible College; where we met and were married later that year, on December 26, 1981 but he's been preaching ever since. And he's given his Testimony wherever we've been, here and abroad, in live meetings and now, through CD's and every form of modern-day, social media and Digital Video available and many people have been healed by just listening to his story! Why?

Because the power of God is always released where there is faith.

Faith moves God...and there are mighty promises when "**We Stand On His Word!**" The Bride-Church will be known by the **DOMINION** she walks in, taking the Authority Christ died to give us, when calamity and trial arise. (Wow)

Mama Purkey lived to the ripe old age of *one hundred years* and was greatly loved and cherished by us all. We all miss her and honor **Minnie Cordia Purkey's** memory here, through this story of her tenacious faith in a Mighty God.

Chapter Nineteen~

DRESSED TO KILL!

"Stay Alert! Watch out for your great enemy,
the devil. He prowls around like a roaring lion,
looking for someone to devour."
(1Peter 5:8) NLV

I like to think of Satan as a roaring lion who has lost all his teeth and has been de-clawed. It helps me put what happened to him, when Jesus rose from the dead, spoiling principalities and powers; in to perspective.

Bride Mentality takes Dominion...*everyday.* We are to subdue our enemy, the devil like a warrior. Jesus has already done the work but we have to "Stay Alert! And *'police things' daily* or we will be taken advantage of. **It's really that simple.** But millions of Christians never do this. They don't pray with authority. *They throw up a "Hail Mary" and hope things go well for them that day.* (Yes, I kid you not....Millions)

Well, guess what? Satan is in the business of making **sure** things **DON'T** go well for us every day. And if we don't subdue him in prayer, *daily binding his attempts and attacks*, loosing the powers of heaven to push open doors of **Favor** for us, (aka: RESISTING him); then it's open season on us. Just look around, he's having a field day with people.

Our **Key Text for All Things Dominion,** is found in Ephesians the sixth chapter. **This is the holy grail of Spiritual Warfare**:

"A final word. Be strong in the Lord and in His mighty power. Put on all of God's armor so that you will be able to stand firm against **all strategies** of the devil. For we are not fighting against flesh and blood enemies, but against evil rulers and authorities of the unseen world, against mighty powers in the dark world and against evil spirits in heavenly places. Therefore, put on every piece of God's armor so you will be able to resist the enemy in the time of evil. Then, after the battle, you will be standing firm. **Stand your ground**, putting on the belt of truth and the body armor of God's righteousness. For shoes, put on the peace that comes from good news so that you will be fully prepared. In addition to all these, hold up the shield of faith to stop the fiery arrows of the devil. Put on salvation as your helmet and take the sword of the Spirit, which is the Word of God." [46] (Emphasis added)

In other words... "We've got To Be Dressed To Kill!"

I first heard that term from our Dear Pastor and Missionary friend, to Rome, Italy, Pastor Francis Santos, whom we have worked with in the faith, for more than twenty five years. He is a General in the Lord's army and I want to give him credit for the phrase I quote here because it's humorous and yet poignant.

Battles that arise are what necessitate spiritual warfare. Conflict in our lives precedes either victory or defeat. It *will* produce one of those. Conflict will not be satisfied any other way. Spiritual warfare transforms our lives into powerful, supernaturally-minded beings, which take Dominion and subdue situations with formidable weapons that have been provided for us to use. Like Mama Purkey, who was in the winter season of her life with physical limitations in her natural body but who became transformed into someone who was mighty in prayer; we too can overcome obstacles and see great answers to our prayers. (Super Like)

Once you get a hold of this... **really get a hold of this**, it will create an insatiable desire to pray with Authority!

In short, Spiritual warfare is addictive.

Addictive, because you can't get enough of how it *really* changes things.

The Bus Stop

I suppose I first learned about spiritual warfare back when I was fifteen years of age. I had to walk a long, tree-lined road to catch my school bus every morning, all by myself. I was afraid of "who" might be in those woods…it was creepy. A relatively new Christian, I told someone at my church about my fears and they provided me with a six-part audio series on Spiritual Authority. I devoured them.

I listened to them morning and night along with one of my favorite books to this day, **Spiritual Authority** , by Watchman Nee. [47] I still have my original copy of it and have referred to this volume often, throughout my life. It was copy written, in 1972, one year before my conversion to Christ and right in the middle of **The Jesus Movement**; I alluded to in Chapter One.

On those dewy morning walks to the bus-stop, down the tree-lined street with tall, skinny Florida pines, I began to recite Ephesians the sixth chapter, and put on the whole armor of God. I realized very quickly that it was a type of covering. Feeling all alone and vulnerable in my single-parent home, I needed something to make me feel more secure. I'm so thankful for the teaching I received on this subject because I could have resorted to many other things to fill my insecurities but God was setting me apart for His purposes, even then. I would pray the same, simple prayer every day, walking up to the Bus Stop. Here's how it went:

"Father, I come to you today in the name of Jesus. I put on the helmet of salvation, so that I can think like you want me to think. Next, I put on the breast-plate of righteousness. I know my own righteous-ness is like a filthy rag but I take upon myself **your** righteousness, Jesus. My waist, I surround with the belt of truth. Lord help me to tell the truth today. I put on the shoes of peace. Help me Lord, to be a peacemaker and to witness to someone today about Jesus. Above all, I take up my shield of faith that will help me quench every fiery dart of Satan and the Word of God which the sword I can stick him with! In Jesus Name, Amen

Now you may be thinking; **seriously**...fifteen years old? As God is my witness, yes. Remember, I'm a survivor. And it was about survival every day for me. I didn't want to go back to smoking pot and cigarettes and being like everyone else I knew in High School. I wanted a better life and when you come from three generations of alcoholism and live in government housing with a single parent on food stamps, etc.; something in all of us **should** want a better way! And I found mine through Jesus Christ. Putting on the Whole Armor of God *(aka: Being Dressed to Kill)*, was my first-step in learning "Who I Am, in Christ" and taking Spiritual Authority.

Can I just tell you? You **Are** someone special. You **Are** powerful. You **Can** walk in Victory. And we **should** be learning about Spiritual Authority and teaching it to our children and grandchildren!

Through Spiritual warfare, we have spiritual EYES. As I said, doing battle in prayer isn't about throwing up a "Hail Mary" and hoping for the best! No, it's about seeing with the *eyes of our Spirit, through the Holy Spirit*; just **where** to attack the enemy and it's about **knowing** our enemy! It's about cutting the legs out from underneath him, with our Sword of the Spirit... God's Holy Word and Standing On the Promises. Sometimes, like our good friends and ministry partners, Ron and Edie Tolbert, of Catoosa, Oklahoma, did; it's about saying *"Enough is Enough, Devil! You can't have my kids!"* and praying those Prodigal sons and daughters back in to the kingdom.

But without **specific** prayer, we are blindly jabbing the enemy and he can dodge us. It's easy for Satan to become a moving target but God's sword of truth is sharp and powerful, able to divide in two, between joint and marrow and is a discerner of the thoughts and intents of the heart. (Heb. 4:12) So when you KNOW God's Word and what is says, you can cut him to the quick with the sword of truth. It's very powerful and we had to do just that, in the story below!

The Gates of Hell on a Paris Metro Train

On January 27, 2014, we were in Paris, France and encountered the spirit under-world as we had never done so before. Traveling on foot, our team, guided by our host church there, entered the underground Metro train station. It is a highly sophisticated network of trains that help in navigating the city and surrounding suburbs of thirteen million Souls. Much more cost-effective than taxis, for larger parties, we opted for the trains.

It was a typical cold, January day in Paris and the icy, north wind made our party of ten, huddle close together for added warmth; as we waited on the embarkation platform, for our routinely crowded train. Its' a mode of transportation that we are usually, quite familiar and comfortable with, in large cities throughout the world; however, there ARE unspoken rules that apply if one wishes to arrive at their destination safely, with valuables intact. After thirty years, of travel, thankfully we know the ropes of being travel savvy on planes, trains and automobiles...*"Keep a Low Profile"*.

"Behold, I send you out as sheep in the midst of wolves. Therefore, be wise as serpents and harmless as doves"; Jesus taught us. [47]

We were unaware that we were "being watched". However, within minutes, it became obvious to several of us that we were being stalked by a group of men, who would not take their eyes off of our two, twenty-something female team members. We boarded our train...so did they. Facing our direction, without even trying to hide their stares, they focused on our two beauty's with an energy that was not just human...it was **demonic.** With cold, steely glares, void of **any** emotion, similar to that of a tiger with its prey, they moved within feet of us on that crowded train.

Keenly aware of Sex trafficking rings throughout the world and especially in large cities like Paris, we have gone right down into the brothels of several major cities, to minister to girls trapped inside the sex-slave trade. However, none of our teams had ever been the direct target of these menaces to society, until this day.

They are vicious, ruthless, cold-blooded killers, who will stop at nothing to trap their prey. Our ladies, now aware of what was going down, were visibly shaken and took their seats. The rest of the team members encircled them, creating a perimeter barrier between them and the salivating stalkers. Bounty is premium for beautiful young women, on the black market of the sex-trade industry…especially American ones and it wasn't your average "fare of the day", on that local Paris Metro train, these evil men were encountering that morning with **our** girls. They were both, truly beautiful. The atmosphere was tense.

*I began praying **OUT LOUD, in the Spirit**, and using the **name of Jesus**.*

Others joined in. We did **not** shut our eyes though, we kept them opened as we prayed and with **Holy Audacity**; staring the devil right back down!

Using the Word, the Name of Jesus and pleading the blood of Jesus, we bound **anything** that could slither, limp, wiggle or walk! The men continued staring, unfazed, never taking their eyes off of our two girls and us, as if they were "sizing up the situation". Some were talking on cell phones to others in the ring. Big money is at stake here and they're playing for keeps. One of our team members looked at the men and said, "NO!" All the while, the train is moving…full of people getting on and off…doors opening, doors closing, making its stops. The tension was excruciating.

After what seemed like an eternity, (it was about 6 stops), the train made a stop and all the men got off and left. We kept praying. Our stop finally arrived and we exited together, as one huddled mass…still praying in the Spirit and using the name of Jesus Christ, the one who "spoiled principalities and powers, making a show of them openly, triumphing over them in it." [48]

We ascended the stairs of the Metro station, to the street for fresh air. Our ladies, so terrorized by the close call, were reduced to tears and vomiting over the nearest trash can, eventually regaining their composure…"*Welcome To Paris!*" *(Note: **never** let **any** young lady or man you care about; go to large cities, unescorted).*

The bottom line…had it not been for our powerful weapons of spiritual warfare, which are not flesh and blood, coupled with a team of people who *knew how to use them,* those team members **would** have fallen prey to the scheme of the devil that day.

The bible says in **1 Peter 5:8** (NLT), *"Satan walks about as a roaring lion, seeking whom he may devour."*

It made such an impact on me personally, that even though I was technically finished writing this book, I added this story during the editing process of the original manuscript because I felt the timing of it all, was divinely orchestrated by God's Spirit, to help lend credibility to the subject of "Taking Dominion." **Touché' Devil.**

Concerning Spiritual Warfare:

The Apostle Paul admonished the Church in this way:

"For though we live in the world, we do not wage war as the world does. The weapons we fight with are not the weapons of the world. On the contrary, they have divine power to demolish strongholds. We demolish arguments and every pretention that sets itself up against the knowledge of God and we take captive every thought to make it obedient to Christ". [50]

My husband and I have a humorous saying that we refer to often, when it seems like we're having a "bad day" and it goes like this:

"Some days you're the windshield and other days you're the bug."

It's funny. But on a serious note, much of what we face in life is because we live in this fallen place. Jesus told us that "on earth, we **would** have trials and sorrows but to take heart, because He had overcome the world."[51]

However, too many Christians get up and get dressed *physically* but **never** get up and get dressed *spiritually* for the day. This immediately makes you "the bug". Why?

It's about being vulnerable.

No one in their right mind would leave their house naked, would they? However, that's exactly what we're doing when we don't pray the Whole Armor of God on us, from Ephesians the sixth chapter. Now, let's look at just "Who" our enemy, Satan is. Allow me to give a little **Back Story** on him, to aid us in "knowing our enemy" for the purposes of "fighting our enemy".

The Archangel, Lucifer and the King of Tyre~

Satan was a great angel, of high ranking, created perfect and good. He was appointed to be a minister at the throne of God; yet sometime **before** the world began, he rebelled and became the chief antagonist of God and man. [52]

The prophet Ezekiel made a proclamation from God against the King of Tyre. Tyre, called "Sour", in Arabic today, was a magnificent and prosperous seaport city. This Old Testament city, along with its sister city, Sidon, are now located in Lebanon, with Tyre twenty miles south of Sidon and only twelve miles north of the Israeli-Lebanese border. Today, each is just a shadow of their former selves. [53]

The King of Tyre's fundamental sin was pride which led him to exalt himself as a deity. For this he would face the judgment of the Lord God and be brought down to the pit, like all mortals (Vs. 8, Ezekiel 28)

Tyre was known for its stunning beauty. Likewise, Satan is depicted as beautiful. In fact, Satan often uses beauty to make his schemes more attractive to us. But beauty can lead to pride, which was Satan and Tyre's downfall. Many today, especially those caught up in New Age thinking or Humanism, actually believe they are their own god, or at least their striving will make them a god. They trust in their own beauty, education, talents, money, etc. to convince themselves of this. However, such deceivers are victims of one of Satan's oldest tricks; in fact, Satan was his own victim of this. It was pride over his own beauty and talent that corrupted him and such deceivers and their victims will receive the same condemnation as the ruler of Tyre.

Listen to this moving passage, depicting the fall of the King of Tyre by paralleling it with the fall of Lucifer:

"Then this further message came to me from the Lord: 'Son of man, sing this funeral song for the King of Tyre. Give him this message from the Sovereign Lord: You were the model of perfection, Full of wisdom and exquisite in beauty. You were in Eden,
The Garden of God. Your clothing was adorned with every precious stone-
Red carnelian, pale green peridot, white moon-stone, blue-green beryl, onyx, green jasper, blue lapis lazuli, turquoise and emerald–
All beautifully crafted for you and set in the finest gold.
They were given to you on the day you were created.

I ordained and anointed you as the mighty angelic guardian.

You had access to the holy mountain of God and walked among the stones of fire. You were blameless in all you did from the day you were created... until evil was found in you.

Your rich (great wealth) commerce filled you with violence, and you sinned.

So, I banished you in disgrace from the mountain of God.

I expelled you, O mighty guardian, from your place among the stones of fire.

Your heart was filled with pride because of all your beauty.

Your wisdom was corrupted by the love of your splendor.

So, I threw you to the ground and exposed you to the curious gaze of kings. You defiled your sanctuaries with your many sins and dishonest trade. So, I brought fire out from within you, and it consumed you. It reduced you to ashes on the ground in the sight of all who were watching.

You have come to a terrible end and you will exist no more". [54]

Holy Moly! It's like an edge-of-your-seat, scene out of a movie...a true one!

Dear Reader, make no mistake Bride Mentality knows her enemy! And the church **knows** she has the Spiritual Authority of God over him *because of how he's been stripped, cast down and spoiled by what Jesus did on the cross. (Amen)*

Who's Dress Are You Wearing?

Through the years, I've enjoyed watching "The Oscars". It's a television program at the beginning of each calendar year that highlights the "Best in Category", in the film and motion picture industry. The Academy Awards Committee work tirelessly for weeks and months on the setting and selections. Everything has to perfect. Inside and out, the venue must shine like pure gold and the people, who are fortunate enough to be invited to the occasion, arrive shimmering in their finest as well. In fact, they are highly critiqued for their appearance.

As the guests arrive, they walk down a red carpet and are greeted by the press. The Question of the night is this:

"Whose dress/suit are you wearing?"

The prevailing societal pressure in our culture today, is to "feel like you've arrived" and are "approved of". This is the essence of the **Pride of Life** and that friends, is the **same** pride that brought Satan down. It's a Major Trap!

A stunning physical appearance, accolades in sports, educational merit, an ornate home, an attractive new car, a new set of clothes—these are all examples of beautiful and valuable things; that in and of themselves are wonderful gifts to us. But they can also make us feel superior to others.

This kind of pride is one of Satan's greatest weapons, because it takes our focus away from WHO we really are and places it upon mere appearances and accomplishments. The pride that can result makes us unattractive to God as well as other people. However, the balance of pride is humility.

Dear Reader, let's use the beautiful things in our lives to welcome people in, not alienate them.

David's prayer of humility in the Psalms is one that we should all pray often:

"Create in me a clean heart O God, Renew a loyal spirit within me. Do not banish me from your presence and don't take your Holy Spirit from me. Restore to me, the joy of your salvation and make me willing to obey you." [55]

10 POINTS OF FACT REGARDING SPIRITUAL WARFARE- [57]

1) The term "world" (in the Greek, "Kosmos"), often refers to the vast system of this age which Satan promotes and which exists independently of God.

   a) Satan is the God of this present world system... he owns it.

   b) Satan (which means "Adversary", in Hebrew), came to Jesus and took him up on a high mountain and showed Jesus all the kingdoms of this world and their glory (or beauty) and said, "If you will bow down and worship me, I'll give it all to you", but Jesus said, "Get thee behind me Satan, for it is written, thou Shalt worship the Lord thy God and Him only shall thy serve." [56]

2) In his rebellion against God, Satan drew with him a great multitude of lesser angels (Rev. 12:4), who are probably to be identified, after the fall, with demons or evil spirits.

3) Satan and many other lesser angels were exiled or cast down to the earth and the atmosphere around it and operate within this sphere under the permissive will of God.

4) Satan also called "the serpent", caused the fall of the human race in the Garden of Eden. (Gen. 3:1-6; 1John 5:19; Luke 13:16; 2Cor 4:4; Gal. 1:4; Eph. 6:12; Heb. 2:14).

   a) The Bible indicates that at the present time, the world is not under God's dominion but is in rebellion against His rule and enslaved by Satan.

   b) Because of this condition, Christ came to die. (John 3:16), and to reconcile the world unto God. (2Cor. 5:18-19).

5) We should never allege that "God is in Control", in order to free ourselves from the responsibility of prayer, serious battling of sin, evil or spiritual Lukewarmness. To just say "Oh, well, God is in Control", when we haven't prayed and are continuing to pray with intense spiritual warfare is to ACCEPT Satan's attack. The lazy man or woman wants to "take the easy way out". **Ease is our Enemy!**

6) Satan's kingdom is a highly systematized empire of evil which has authority over the lower heavenly

realm (Eph. 2:2), fallen angels (Rev. 12:1), and the world (Luke 4:5-6; 2Cor. 4:4; 1John 5:19). I say unregenerated because he does **not** have control over the child of God! Jesus broke those chains for us!

7) He is **not** omnipresent (present everywhere), omnipotent (all powerful) or omniscient (all knowing), therefore, most of his activity is delegated to demons. (Matt. 8:28; Rev. 16:13-14; Job 1:12).

8) Jesus came to earth to destroy the works of Satan. (1John 3:8); Establish the Kingdom of God and deliver us from Satan's dominion. (Matt.12:28; Luke 4:18, 13:16, Acts 26:18). By His death and resurrection, Christ initiated the defeat of Satan and thereby ensured God's ultimate victory over him. (Heb. 2:14).

9) Satan presently wars against God and His people (Job 1:2; Eph. 6:11-18), seeking to draw them away from loyalty to Christ (2 Cor. 11:3) and lure them into sin and this present world system. (1 Tim. 5:15; 1 John 5:16). The believer is to pray constantly for deliverance:

a) from temptation (Matt. 6:13)

b) to be on the alert concerning his schemes and attacks (Eph. 6:11)

c) And to resist him by spiritual warfare while remaining firm in the faith. (Eph. 6:10-18; 1Pet. 5:8-9).

10) Finally, Satan has a time limit!

a) At the end of the age, Satan is confined to the abyss for a thousand years. (Rev. 20:1-3).

After his release, he will make a final attempt to overthrow God; this will result in Satan's irrevocable defeat and his being cast into the lake of fire. (Rev. 20:7-10).

(Ah Hem), **as I said, I like to think of Satan as a roaring lion with no teeth, who has been de-clawed!**

The Scarlet Thread~

When our children were little, I used to take a spool of red thread and cut it in to little pieces. I would tape a piece of that red thread to the top of all the door frames in our house. We moved a lot in our early ministry but each time we relocated, I would repeat this act. No one knew the thread was there but God and I...*and the devil.*

I would pray a simple prayer of Spiritual Authority over our home and our family. Here is my simple prayer:

"Father, I come in the name of Jesus, using these little pieces of red thread as a symbol of the blood that Jesus shed for our lives, on the cross; blood that was shed for us to have and enjoy peace and protection from the enemy.

So Lord, just as the children of Israel sprinkled the blood of a Sacrificial lamb over the doorposts of their homes, so that evil would pass over them; I pray that you would honor my faith through these pieces of red thread that: **No Weapon that would be formed against our family would prosper and that anyone, or anything that would rise up against my children, my marriage or our home, would fail.** *In Jesus Name, Amen"*

Friends, this prayer is *powerful*! And it has proven to be very effective for over thirty years, no matter where we have lived. I have adapted it from my sister-in law, Pastor Mary Purkey, of Lenexa Christian Center, in Lenexa, Kansas, who is a mighty prayer warrior and who also prayed this over their homes, wherever they lived. Today, both of her sons, Matthew and Jonathan Purkey, are now preaching the Gospel of our Lord Jesus Christ. This concept is based on the scripture passage below from **Exodus 12:23.** I encourage you to use it!

"For the Lord will pass through the land to strike the Egyptians but when He sees the blood on the top and sides of the door frame, the Lord will pass over your home. He will not permit his death angel to enter your house and strike you down."

Are we using all the Spiritual Authority given to us through Christ? Probably not. *Bride Mentality is Warfare Mentality*. **Use Your Weapons!**

Whenever calamity arises in your job, family or personal health, it's time to go to prayer and "call Satan out"! Prayer moves the heavenlies. Spiritual warfare is some of the most intense work you'll ever do...I learned *that* praying for my alcoholic, demon oppressed father for fifteen years. But in the end, Satan **must** surrender to the name of Jesus and quoted scripture from God's Holy Word. Blow by blow, with every passage the child of God stands on, you systematically cut the legs out from underneath him.

We can use our spiritual authority to combat **many** different forms of resistance that we come up against. *(My companion Study-Guide will take you on a journey of areas of your life with which you can apply Spiritual Authority).*

Here is a list of examples:

- Praying for unsaved loved ones to come to Christ.
- Physical attack on your body, or those you love.
- Depression/Suicide
- Fear of Anything – (1 Tim. 1:7)

  Doom, Dread, Death

  Fear of Disapproval

  Fear of Being Controlled

  Fear of Losing Control

  Fear of heights, crowds, being alone, etc.
- Generational Curses – of poverty, addiction, sexual or substance abuse, witchcraft/ occult, etc.
- Persecution of your Christian Faith on your job, from your family or in your ministry (i.e. Missionaries, etc.)
- From Drifting and becoming Luke-warm and Apathetic towards the things of God and in love with this world (Bridezilla).
- From following the desires of the sinful nature, which result in sexual immorality, impurity, lustful pleasures, idolatry, sorcery, hostility, quarreling, jealousy, outbursts of anger, selfish ambition, dissention, division, envy, drunkenness, wild parties and the like. (Gal. 5:21).

GIVING – THE SECRET WEAPON!

Finally, there is another powerful tool in our arsenal of weaponry and it is a bit of a *secret weapon*. Its' extremely productive though, in putting the enemy to flight, and if used under the leading of the Holy Spirit; it **WILL** put the enemy to flight. It is none other than **GIVING.**

Jesus likens Satan to a thief who comes to steal, kill and destroy. But said, "Remember, I came to give you life more abundantly". [58]

One of the first things that occur in the life of a new believer, are the blessings of God that begin to take place. It's a wonderful thing! God blesses His children and supplies their needs, as they submit to Him and begin to do a one-eighty in life-style and behavior. God loves to bless obedience. But the "rub" comes in **here** because Satan is not happy about that and will begin to attack our finances (provision), through our jobs, the world's economy, an attack on our physical bodies or a menagerie of other things. Believe me; we know he will try to steal **everything** the Lord gives us!

So what can we do?

Outsmart him by Giving to Missions (Souls)!

Seriously. We've proven this time-honored tactic for over thirty years. Each time we receive negative news regarding our health, our job (our ministry), etc.; we would increase our giving to Missions by a love offering... even if it was only a few dollars. No matter how large or how small, supporting missionaries is like sweet incense on the altar of God. Why?

Because lost Souls are the heart beat of God.

It's absolutely true. Its' what God longs for—lost humanity coming to Jesus Christ. Those who are involved in full-time 24/7 Evangelism like Christian Missionaries and Missionary Evangelists, take the gospel to the Lost People of this world. Supporting them will open the hand of God to you and your family and will put "Buck-Shot" in the devil's "Back-Side!" (Here's to clinking my coffee cup with you now).

I challenge you to try it next time calamity of any kind arises. Our son, Luke and his wife, Andrea have already learned this secret in the short time they have been married and have shared testimonies with us, of how these principles are working in their family and of their plans to teach it to their children! It is so rewarding, as parents, to see Spiritual Warfare passing to the next generation of the Bride-Church!

Teach these principles to your children and grandchildren!

Christ has promised that His authority, power and presence will accompany us as we battle the kingdom of Satan. (Matt. 28:18-20; Luke 24:47-49). We must liberate people from their captivity by preaching and sharing the gospel **(Compassion),** *like the "Pie Lady"*, by living a righteous life (Matt. 6:33; Rom. 6:13; 14:17) and by performing **Signs and Miracles through the Power of the Holy Spirit and prayer**, *like "Mama Purkey"*. Don't keep this secret to yourself (I'm not!) Share It!

These spiritual manifestations are intended to continue within Christ's church until Jesus Returns! The scripture never suggested that these signs were restricted to the early church only (the period immediately after his ascension). (1Cor. 1:7; 12:28; Gal. 3:5). It is clear that we are to not only share the Gospel of the kingdom and bring salvation to those who believe but to cast out demon spirits, (like I saw in my father), and pray for healing and miracles for those with sickness and diseases, (like my husband, Mark experienced).

There is truly Freedom in Jesus, when we're Dressed to Kill!

Chapter Twenty~

THE TORNADO, THE SEMI-TRUCK AND THE UNSEEN HAND

"The hammers of life come to everyone but it's how we respond to them that determines victory or defeat."

Pastor Jim McNabb

The Bridge Church, Mustang, OK

*I*t was a normal windy Saturday in March of 1996. This time of the year, here in the Central plains, means **Tornado Season** is fast approaching and in this part of the U.S., we don't play around with Mother Nature. Especially our family, we live in Mustang, Oklahoma which is approximately twenty miles from Moore, Oklahoma... the *epicenter* for "the most destructive tornados on the planet". *EF4 and EF5, we've seen them all, more than once and they're deadly.*

My husband was loading the car that morning to drive to his next meeting, in Dodge City, Kansas. It would be a week-long, Spiritual Emphasis meeting with a church that he had ministered in several times before. So, he was familiar with the driving route. We all hugged and kissed good-bye and I stayed back with our baby daughter, Lyndi who was just a year old and with our son, Luke, who was in grade school at the time. Without a cloud in the sky, Mark left, promising to call us upon his arrival. We were all used to this scenario, as Missionary Evangelists.

As he traveled north on Interstate 35 out of Oklahoma City, toward Wichita, Kansas, he exited on Highway 160, West, just past the Oklahoma border and noticed the sky had darkened. Proceeding further, it wasn't long before he saw a Wall Cloud. "What in the world?" he thought to himself. Deteriorating rapidly, the weather turned violent and big drops of pelting rain hit his windshield, making visibility difficult. That's when he saw it.

The flashing red and blue lights of the Kansas Highway Patrol, who had closed down the Interstate, just a few miles ahead. In the distance, a funnel cloud was visible. "Goodness gracious", he muttered to himself. "Lord please help me to get to my meeting!"

Back home, I was tuned into the weather station and saw trouble ahead for my husband. Calling his mobile phone, I said, "Mark, you're headed directly towards a tornado on the ground, turn around!" He quickly agreed but then immediately followed by saying, "I can't! There's another one right behind me!" his voice shaking. He hung up the phone to concentrate and I immediately went to the couch in our den and hit my knees. I began to fight spiritual warfare in prayer there, as Mark did behind the wheel of his rental car.

Left with no options, Mark took the last available exit before coming to the closed Interstate 35. He went West and North, West and North, West and North, with absolutely no idea where he was, since it was an unmarked Farm Road. The rain was coming down in torrents. Pounding hail began. It was deafening inside the rental car, hitting the hood, top and sides like baseballs. Mark thought the glass might break. He had been praying fervishly all along but just then, He felt the Lord speak to him something very unexpected.

"HOLD UP YOUR HAND."

"Hold up my hand? What does that mean?" Mark wondered to himself. Still, he felt a definite direction from the Lord to hold up his hand like it was "cupped" over something. So, feeling silly and really glad no one was around to see it, (Insert wink here), **he obeyed**. He felt the Lord tell him to *"Proceed"*. Out of options, he held up one hand and with the other, gripped the steering wheel and proceeded down the soaked Farm Road, bumping along as he rolled over pieces of ice the size of golf, tennis and baseballs!

Praying with his hand up, in the pounding hail and rain, he continued driving West and North, West and North, West and North until finally, the rain stopped. It was the first clearing he'd had in several hours and he suddenly realized how tired and stiff his body felt from gripping the wheel so tightly. His neck and shoulders ached.

Getting out of his rental car, a sick feeling came over him. He realized it would be a total loss and that he would have to pay for it. However, to his utter shock and amazement, as he inspected the hood, roof and sides of the car, *there wasn't a single dent or ping of hail damage*! (But God)

Suffice to say, there was "a little church" **had** that day, by a traveling preacher, alongside that Kansas black top road! (Yes, I kid you not)

As God instructed my husband to hold up his hand, simultaneously, God held up His mighty hand over the little car. It was truly miraculous. And when he was able, he got back into the car and drove just a little further, before he came to a directional sign. It read, **Minneola, Kansas 21 miles.** Minneola is just south of Dodge City *and as you can probably imagine, the little Church there had a GREAT Revival that week!*

The Semi-Truck and the Unseen Hand~

I love praise and worship music, especially in my car! But I'll never forget the day *"Praise Saved Us!"*

My children Luke and Lyndi (age twelve and four, respectively, at that time), were with me in our 1999, Ford Expedition. We were headed home from Toys R Us and a special lunch outing…just the three of us. We had our "praise on" and the music was cranked up and we were all singing to the Lord. It seemed like God was right in the car with us, His presence was so beautifully real. Such a sweet memory, well, sort of...

Traveling on Interstate 240 in Oklahoma City, I veered over to the far left lane to exit Airport Road, in the direction of our home. A semi-truck was next to me, a few feet ahead, in the right lane. Suddenly! I saw his left directional signal go on, but I wasn't ahead of him yet...he was coming over on top of us! I "gunned" the accelerator to try and get ahead of him knowing instinctively, that his great size put my SUV at a disadvantage and we could roll over. Getting ahead of him was the shortest distance to clearing the truck, however; *to our horror his front bumper hit the back of our Ford Expedition,* **before** *I could get ahead of him*. Terrified, we felt our back tires lift off of the pavement.

We were hooked together and the semi was now pushing us ahead going no less than 65 miles an hour!

Instinctively, I cried out on the name of the Lord. "Jesus, Save Us!" I yelled. With the praise music still going, we drifted along, like we were floating, for several seconds before I felt a distinctive **"jolt"** from behind.

"It felt like we came unhooked", I thought. We Were!

With my hands and body shaking, I managed to coast the SUV to the shoulder of the road and came to a complete stop. Stunned, we sat there in disbelief, trying to wrap our minds around what had just occurred. The trucker did the same, however, slowly; he got out of his cab. Approaching us, I could see him in my side-view mirror, take off his seed-grain, ball cap and scratch his head. He surveyed *his* front bumper and *our* rear one before coming alongside my driver's window. Shaking his head, he sputtered, *"You alright, M'am?"* Before I could answer, he continued, *"I never even saw you…I thought we were 'Goners' for sure; before we came unhooked. Guess we just got lucky."*

Lucky? I think not. I don't believe "Luck" had **anything** to do with it. I believe Satan tried to kill my family and I that day but Praise put him to flight, spoiling his plans.

Did you know that Praise moves the Hand of God? It does.

Satan hates praise and worship because it reminds him of why he was created and what he gave up. *Satan **must** flee when we praise the name of Jesus!* This **is** spiritual warfare as much as any of the other methods, I've outlined. *Be sure you're using the Mighty Weapon of Praise!*

~~~BRIDE MENTALITY~~~
COMPENDIUM~

Bride or Bridezilla?

What NOT to Wear

I suppose every little boy dreams of being a Super-hero and every little girl dreams of being Cinderella. And in The Bride of Christ, we have a little of both.

"But you are a chosen people, a royal priesthood, a holy nation, God's special possession, that you may declare the praises of Him who called you out of darkness into His wonderful light. [59]

I can't help but wonder how many of us have a God-dream inside of us but we're so afraid of failure, we never even try? We have a natural propensity to fear, you know. Worry-filled days, ball-of-barbed wire in your stomach, that all-too-familiar "moods" and self-guessing... It all works AGAINST your leadership and being All God wants us to be!

There are two things that set "Dreamers" apart from "Doers".
1) **Deed Execution** – sometimes you just have to "go for it." Nike had it right.
2) **Obedience** – God doesn't give us a new assignment until we've finished strong on the previous one.

236

- So, is there anything in your life gathering the *"dust of disobedience?"* Heaven can get awfully quiet when we're not obeying.

This book... for ME, wasn't just about becoming a published Author. It was an act of *OBEDIENCE* and an exercise in *DEED EXECUTION* and can I make a confession here? Part of me was afraid to write it. I'm a Vocalist, I reasoned, I need to stay in my box! But I pressed through that wall of resistance with this Prayer:

"Command me to write, Lord God! Gift me. If this is something you are leading me to do, I take the limits off of *myself*. I reach out and receive your good gift of "equipping". It's mine! I take it! I take dominion over my fears. I **will** write what God has put in my heart to write. Let your Favor fall on me! I **will** Follow my Favor and gifting, so that I can hear two all-important words: **"Well Done!"** (Amen)

And that was my turning point, another defining life moment. Now, I see "**POISED With Bride Mentality**", as a "laying on of hands, so-to-speak, to stir the gifts up, out there, in the body of Christ. God wants to stir-up the gifts that are lying dormant in His Bride Church and I have prayed that He would use my book to do it! This is body ministry. Don't be like the "Pie Lady" in Chapter Six and say you don't have any gifts or talents. That's like burying them in the sand and God won't let us get away with that. He'll call us out on it and label us a wicked and slothful servant! **So, how about you?**

- **Do you have a secret dream that God has put in your heart and gifted you to accomplish?**
- **What are you doing with that?**

You can't just pray over your God-whispers, you know. You will have to take your thoughts (God-ideas), captive and at some point, stop praying (and start sweating) to make them realities!

Remember, Deed Execution IS Obedience.

I tend to be a Personality Profiler and have found that creative people often struggle with the curse of perfectionism and Satan will use that against us. The devil will try to pooh-pooh everything you attempt to do with voices of doubt and discouragement in your mind or from people. In fact, he'll use the people right around you, to discourage you the most, sometimes. Don't accept those voices!

Cast them down just like God casted him down. Satan has been discredited and disavowed. He broke rank and gave up the best "GIG" you could ever hope for...God's anointed, covering Cherub that led heaven in Holy worship on God's Holy Mountain. Talk about the total package... are you kidding me? Satan had it! No, he's like the movie, *"Dumb and Dumber."* We can walk all over him with the Word of God (the Bible).

Church-Brides everywhere, we can be dressed to kill and rock 'in our spiritual heels, all over him!

Use the weapons of your warfare. Get your ammo ready and shoot straight! Get him right between his beady eyes with **Scripture, Giving and Praise!**

Know **who** and **Whose** you are, Dear Reader!

We Are: the Bride of Christ and we are P.O.I.S.E.D.!
- Powerful in **Prayer**
- **Obedient** to His Voice
- Living lives of personal **Integrity**
- Well-**Studied** in His Love Letters
- **Eyes Focus**ed on our Lover, Jesus the Bridegroom
- And Taking **Dominion** over the devil in this fallen place with no Apology!

And that, Dear Reader, is *Staying* **POISED with Bride Mentality!**

Be Ready! Keep Watching!
Never Run Out of Oil!

<u>Be Ready For the Lord's Coming</u>

"Be dressed for service and keep your lamps burning, as though you were waiting for your master to return from the wedding feast. Then you will be ready to open the door and let Him in, the moment He arrives and knocks. The servants who are ready and waiting for His return will be rewarded. I tell you the truth, He himself will seat them, put on an apron and serve them as they sit and eat! He may come in the middle of the night or just before dawn, but when He comes, He will reward the servants who are ready. You also must be ready all the time, for the Son of Man will come when least expected." (Luke 12:35-38 NLT)

END NOTES

1. **"The Human Genome Project Completion, Frequently Asked Questions".** National Human Genome Research Institute. http://www.genome.gov /11006943. Updated

2. Jeremiah 29:11 (NLT)

3. Luke 6:46 (NLT)

4. Wikipedia, **Jesus Movement** en.wikipedia.org/wiki/ Jesus_movement
   Also: www.one-way.org/jesusmovement

5. John 14:2 & 3 (NLT)

6. The National Center for Family and Marriage Research (2010). Divorce Rate in the U.S. (2008). (http://ncfmr.bgsu.edu/family2008.pdf)
   Schoen, R. , Canudas-Romo, V. (2006) Timing effects on divorce:20th Century experienced in the United States. Journal of Marriage and family, 68, 749-758.

US Census Bureau (2009) Current Population Survey, 2009 Annual Social and Economic Supplement. (http://www.census.gov/population/www/socdemo/ hh-fam/cps2009.html)

US Census Bureau (2010). Statistical Abstract of the United States: 2010 (129th Edition), Washington, DC. (http://www.census.gov/statub/www/)

7. Luke 5:16 (NLT)
8. Matthew 9:15 (NLT)
9. Isaiah 61:3 (NLT)
10. Romans 8:13 (NLT)
11. Matthew 6:17 -18 (NLT)
12. References used in the Fasting Session are:

Fast Your Way To Health, Lee Bueno-Aquer (1991 Whitaker House)

Preparing for the Coming Revival, Bill Bright (1995 New Life Publications),

The Transforming Power of Fasting and Prayer, Bill Bright (1997 NLP)

A Common Sense Guide to Fasting, Kenneth E. Hagin (1981 Faith Library Publications).

13. Philippians 2:12,& 13 (NLT)
14. Deuteronomy 30: 15-16 (NLT)
15. John 14:15-17, 21 (NLT)

16. 1 Samuel 15:22 (NLT)

17. Luke 6:46 (NLT)

18. Psalms 95:8 (NLT)

19. Proverbs 28:13 (NLT)

20. **All The Parables of the Bible,** Lockyer, 1963 Zondervan

21. **The Parables of the Kingdom**, G. Campbell Morgan, Hodder & Soughton, London, 1960

22. **R.C. Trench,The Parables of our Lord**, Kegan Paul, Trench & Company, London, 1889

23. **The Parables of Jesus**, George A. Butterick, Harper & Brothers, New York, 1928.

24. Ecclesiastes 12:13-14 (NLT)

25. Joshua 1:8 (NLT)

26. **Primal, A Quest for the Lost Soul of Christianity**, Mark Batterson, Multnomah Books, Colorado Springs, CO, 2009

27. **Excerpt from article in Enrichment Magazine: Believing God for a Prophetically Relevant Church**, by Doug Clay, General Treasurer, Assemblies of God, Springfield, MO, 2013.

28. 2 Timothy 2:15 (Amplified Bible)

29. Psalms 119:11 (NLT)

30. Revelation 21:21 (NLT)

31. 1 Corinthians 2:9 &10 (NLT)

32. **Excerpt from article in Enrichment Magazine: "The Believer's Eye"**, by David Paul Applegate, Arlington, Texas, 2013

33. Mark 13:33-37 (NLT)

34. 1 Peter 5:8 (NLT)

35. Ephesians 5:25-27 (NLT)

36. Psalms 45:10-11; 13-17 (NLT)

37. **The Study of Parables**, Ada R. Habershon, Pickering & Inglis, London, n.d.

38. Ephesians 5:25b-27 (NLT)

39. Jeremiah 32:40 (NLT)

40. Jeremiah 3:1-4 (NLT)

41. Isaiah 44:18, 19 (NLT)

42. 2 Timothy 3:1-5 (NLT)

43. Ezekiel 11:19-20 (NLT)

44. **"Standing On The Promises"**, Written by R. Kelso Carter, 1849-1928.

45. Isaiah 53:4-5 (NLT)

46. Ephesians 6:10-17 (NLT)

47. **Spiritual Authority**, Watchman Nee, Christian Fellowship Publishers, Inc. New York, 1972

(Add'l. note: The contents of this volume comprise a series of messages which were delivered in Chinese by the author during a training period for workers held in Kuling, Foochow, China, in 1948, and are now translated from the edited notes taken by some who attended that training).

48. Matthew 10:16 (NKJV)

49. Colossians 2:15 (KJV)

50. 2 Corinthians 10:3-5 (NIV)

51. John 16:33 (NLT)

52. Ezekiel 28:12-15 (NLT)

53. **Tyre Through the Ages** , Jidejian, N. Beirut Librairie Orientale, 1996.

54. Ezekiel 28:11-19 (NLT)

55. Psalm 51:10-12 (NLT)

56. Matthew 4:10 (KJV)

57. **Study Note on: The Christian's Relationship with the World (pg. 2004)**. Donald C. Stamps, M.A. M.DIV. The New Life Study Bible (aka: The Fire Bible), Zondervan Publishing House, Grand Rapids, MI, 1992.

58. John 10:10 (NLT)

59. 1 Peter 2:9 (NLT)

ABOUT THE AUTHOR

*F*or more than 30 years, Susan Purkey (Susie), along with her husband, Mark and their 2 children have been full-time, Missionary Evangelists and International Speakers with the Assemblies of God; traveling throughout the US and Europe holding City-wide Crusades and Conferences. They are presently ministering in over 20 foreign countries and have preached the Gospel of Jesus Christ to over 1.5 Million people and have seen more than 100,000 Souls won to Christ.

Susie is a Credentialed Minister with the Assemblies of God and a 1982 Graduate of Central Bible College, in Springfield, Missouri where she obtained a B.A. in Vocal Music Performance and a Minor in Biblical Studies. She is a gifted Speaker, with a dramatic Back Story, recounted in this book, Mentor, Vocal Music Instructor and anointed Recording Artist, with 6 Music CD's to her credit and now, finally a Published Author!

Susie resides in the Oklahoma City area with her husband, children and 2 grandchildren, who know her affectionately as "Nina".

FURTHER PRODUCT AND CONTACT INFORMATION

Susie Purkey Music CD's & Mark Purkey's Healing Testimony CD are available for purchase at:
www.MarkPurkey.com

Companion Study-Guide:
POISED With Bride Mentality
Ideal for individual or Church Groups: Available Summer, 2014 from Xulon Press and
wherever fine books are sold.

For Future Bookings – Our mailing address is:
Mark Purkey Ministries, Inc.
P.O. Box 211
Mustang, Oklahoma 73064
or www.MarkPurkey.com

CPSIA information can be obtained at www.ICGtesting.com
Printed in the USA
LVOW06s1124170414

382096LV00001B/1/P

9 781629 521404